Ears to Proclaim God's Splendor

ACTIVATING SPIRITUAL HEARING THROUGH SONG

Zolisha L Ware

Copyright © 2020 by **Zolisha L Ware**

All rights reserved. No part of this publication may be reproduced, distributed or transmitted in any form or by any means, including photocopying, recording, or other electronic or mechanical methods, without the prior written permission of the publisher, except in the case of brief quotations embodied in critical reviews and certain other noncommercial uses permitted by copyright law. For permission requests, write to the publisher, addressed "Attention: Permissions Coordinator," at the address below.

Zolisha L Ware/Rejoice Essential Publishing
PO BOX 512
Effingham, SC 29541
www.republishing.org

Unless otherwise indicated, scripture is taken from the King James Version.'

All Scripture quotations are taken from THE MESSAGE, copyright © 1993, 2002, 2018 by Eugene H. Peterson. Used by permission of NavPress, represented by Tyndale House Publishers. All rights reserved.

Scripture quotations marked (NIV) are taken from the Holy Bible, New International Version®, NIV®. Copyright © 1973, 1978, 1984, 2011 by Biblica, Inc.™ Used by permission of Zondervan. All rights reserved worldwide. www.zondervan.com The "NIV" and "New International Version" are trademarks registered in the United States Patent and Trademark Office by Biblica, Inc.™

New American Standard NEW AMERICAN STANDARD BIBLE Copyright (C) 1960, 1962, 1963, 1968, 1971, 1972, 1973, 1975, 1977,1995 by THE LOCKMAN FOUNDATION A Corporation Not for Profit LA HABRA, CA All Rights Reserved http://www.lockman.org

Scripture quotations marked HCSB are taken from the Holman Christian Standard Bible®, Used by Permission HCSB ©1999,2000,2002,2003,2009 Holman Bible Publishers. Holman Christian Standard Bible®, Holman CSB®, and HCSB® are federally registered trademarks of Holman Bible Publishers.

The Holy Bible, Berean Study Bible, BSBCopyright ©2016, 2018 by Bible Hub Used by Permission. All Rights Reserved Worldwide.

Scripture taken from the New King James Version®. Copyright © 1982 by Thomas Nelson. Used by permission. All rights reserved.

The Holy Bible, English Standard Version (ESV) is adapted from the Revised Standard Version of the Bible, copyright Division of Christian Education of the National Council of the Churches of Christ in the U.S.A. All rights reserved.

All Scripture marked with the designation "GW" is taken from GOD'S WORD®. © 1995, 2003, 2013, 2014, 2019, 2020 by God's Word to the Nations Mission Society. Used by permission.

Ears to Proclaim God's Splendor/Zolisha L Ware

ISBN-13: 978-1-952312-58-8
Library of Congress Control Number: 2021902613

Table of Contents

ACKNOWLEDGMENT..vii
PREFACE..vii
INTRODUCTION..1
    Activation Exercise #1..4
    Activation Exercise #2..5
LESSON 1:   Hear..13
    Activation 1:   Spirit of the Lord Fill this Room...........22
    Activation 2:   We Need You Today..............................28
    Activation 3:   Prince of Peace......................................35
    Activation 4:   Praise Your Name..................................42
    Activation 5:   Worthy Praise...48
LESSON 2:   Heard..55
    Activation 6:   Righteous One..63
    Activation 7:   I Need More..70
    Activation 8:   You Tried It..76
    Activation 9:   This Is How..83
    Activation 10: Glory..90
LESSON 3:   Hearer..98
    Activation 11: Let It Be Me...100
    Activation 12: I'm Blessed..109
    Activation 13: Oh, How I Worship You.....................118
    Activation 14: I Shall Decree.......................................124
    Activation 15: Blessed It Be the Child.........................130
LESSON 4:   Hearest...137
    Activation 16: We Worship 139
    Activation 17: Bless It Be the Lord..............................146
    Activation 18: Teach Us!...152

    Activation 19: The Anchor of My Soul........................159
    Activation 20: Love...165
LESSON 5:   Heareth..171
    Activation 21: Fall on Me...173
    Activation 22: You Got to Go!....................................180
    Activation 23: Take Your Place..................................186
    Activation 24: Bow Down & Worship........................192
    Activation 25: Mark Me..198
LESSON 6:   Hearing..204
    Activation 26: Crush It..206
    Activation 27: Greater is He.......................................213
    Activation 28: Greater is Coming...............................219
    Activation 29: I Will Trust...225
    Activation 30: One Touch...231
LESSON 7:   Hearken...239
    Activation 31: I Will..241
    Activation 32: Secret Place...248
    Activation 33: Send Your Presence............................254
    Activation 34: Loose Your Favor................................260
    Activation 35: Shake Us 267
LESSON 8:   Hearkeneth..274
    Activation 36: Matchless Savior.................................275
    Activation 37: For You Loved Me...............................282
    Activation 38: The Sound...290
    Activation 39: God is Big..297
    Activation 40: Knock Out...304
CONCLUSION...310
ABOUT THE AUTHOR..313
NOTES..317

Acknowledgment

To the lover of my soul, Christ Jesus, who saved me and asked the Father God to send the Holy Spirit unto me. He opened my ears to hear things beyond this world that I may teach others to walk according to the spirit and not their physical being, that heaven may become a familiar and understood sound to all who desire to have ears to hear.

Preface

HAVE YOU EVER EXPERIENCED a time in your life that no words could help you? No matter what's said, the pain would not go away. You tried to pray, but nothing. You asked others to pray but nothing. Then you heard a song that spoke to your heart. The words of the song had a melody of healing, deliverance, and breakthrough. The music shifts your mood, spirit, mind and heart. These are not just any songs but prophetic songs from Heaven. That penetrates your heart and brings life to your soul. The Apostle John teaches us in Revelations 19:10 that worship is the spiritual breath of Heaven, and it speaks to the testimony of Jesus because prophecy is the very spirit of Christ. Prophecy is the testimony of Christ. Jesus came to restore the past, establish our present, and bring a more splendid future that we cannot have without Him. Being married unto Christ opens us up to things beyond this world. The devil tries to make these things fearful or impossible because we are in a corruptible world.

Marriage unto Christ destroys the fear and brings in a force of faith that brings with it access unto things our physical bodies cannot comprehend. That is further clarified in Revelation

22:8, And I am John, who heard and saw these things. And when I had heard and seen them, I fell down to worship at the feet of the angel who had shown me these things. Once John heard Heaven and saw, his understanding was opened significantly. He wrote the Book of the Revelation that we may listen that our knowledge would be open. That is the power of sound from Heaven. The sound of Heaven is nothing new. It is discussed in the Bible many times and is often overlooked. You have the Songs of Solomon, which is a display of a man's love for a woman. Then you have the Psalms that are songs from various people in the Bible that foretold through music, prophecy, poems, and hymns depicting their sorrow and ways the Lord would deliver them or even how they loved their God. The Word Psalms in Hebrew means song or poems. The definition of Psalms is a sacred song or poem used in worship ((n.d), 2020).

Add the unction of heaven upon that song, and you have a glory that will blow you beyond anything your mind can fathom. Revelations 22:17 states the spirit and the bride say, "Come!" Let the one who hears say, "Come!" And let the one who is thirsty come and the one who desires the water of life drink freely. Jesus is coming. Will you hear Him when He is on the way, or will you have to wait until He appears unto all the world. To listen to the Lord is beyond hearing what is within this world. Your spirit man has to be awakened and connected to the Lord. Although you are physically on this earth, you have access to another location beyond any chronological time. It is beyond what you physically see. Within John 14:20, John reminds us of the teaching of Christ when He told them, "At that day you will know that I am in My Father, and you in Me, and I in you." That day happens when you begin to experience things that you can't accomplish in your strength, nor have you heard of it in this world. Having all our senses open is very important. Within this book, we focus on activating our hearing.

Hearing is necessary as a believer. If we are supposed to speak affirmations and proclamations that we are established and only have access to the written Word, we are limited to what God wants to do in our lives and those around us.

Introduction

THE LORD SPEAKS TO us in so many different ways. Most focus on hearing His soft still voice that when He sends something loud and clear, we deny that it is the Lord at all. There are no limitations to hearing the splendor of our Lord. Our rules come by way of ourselves. Most don't understand that the Lord is waiting to respond to our request. Like us, He doesn't like being talked at, nor does He want to be misunderstood, which is why He gave us His Word and His Son Jesus. That we may gain truth not merely based on just what we read but what we heard directly out of Jesus' mouth. There are over ninety-six verses of Scripture in the Bible about hearing. Most people in relationships with God spend more time talking than listening, which causes them to lose vital information. It is time to stop losing essential information and gain valuable insight that will bring you closer to the Father than you ever imagine.

I often find myself spending more time on things about God than the things of this world. I no longer desire this world's music, no matter if it is said to praise God. I hope to live a Spirit-filled life dead unto my carnal nature but alive unto the Glory of the Lord that it may overtake me and show me godly reverences that will draw out those who hear the Word of the Lord but destroy those who forbear Ezekiel 3:11. Some would say that is a hard statement, but that is what it truly will take for us to be as Romans 12:1 has directed. We can't be of this world and of God's world that is called double-mindedness. Our goal is to be the influencers, not influenced. To effectively control once must be under the influence.

Under the influence of the Holy Spirit, that will lead to all truth. A truth that will show you things you never thought possible; however, you obtain them because you went beyond this world and over into the high places given unto us by way of the blood of Christ. Thus, I find myself being like Ezekiel, where God had to place him on his feet to eat because he spent all his time in the high places within Glory. Ezekiel 2 & 3—allowing the Lord to feed words of instruction that housed healing, deliverance, and position. Many of us cannot hear the words because we haven't completed the first thing: dying unto ourselves. I was stuck once this way stuck in brokenness, shame, and rejection; however, it was the music from heaven that awakened me in the night. The sound didn't just awaken me naturally but spiritually, understanding that this world was not in control and that if I learned how to stay within the presence of the Lord, the enemy would not be able to trace me.

Taking the biblical Word as living, and my life is hidden within Christ God (Colossians 3:3), I closed myself to the dead things of this world and set residence in God's Kingdom. Once I accepted this concept when under attack, I would begin to hear

Introduction

music. Once I would listen to music and speak what I heard. My way of escape would appear. The Lord would make a way out of no way right before me (Philippians 2:13,14 and Isaiah 43:16-19). I learned that music was my way to freedom. Thus, when the enemy would come in like a flood, I would raise the standard by opening my mouth and singing what I heard. Sometimes it would start with Scripture or just a simple prayer; however, the Lord would give me a song every time. Once the song came, I would experience the presence of God like no other. I begin to experience "Great things!" I began to see what the Lord had promised because I had accessed a door that no man could shut. The prophetic song gave me entry that the enemy is denied because it possesses the Glory of the Lord that all of the heavens turn to usher in Glory that nothing evil can stand and nothing broken can stay broken within. As I heard the worship and music of Heaven, my thinking changed. It was this music that got me through my time of brokenness. Every time I get into a hard place, the Lord would tell me the song needed to receive my breakthrough.

Regardless of the song, the more I sang what I heard, the more things would line up. No matter if I'm under attack by people, places, or something, the Lord will show me the source of the attack, and as I sing the song the Lord gives me, the enemy has to flee because God inhabits the praises of His people (Psalm 22:3). Within this book, you will learn how to proclaim God's splendor out of your mouth. You will learn how to hear beyond what's typically heard. Receiving a more significant power source transforming your life directly from the courts of praise.

Ears to Proclaim God's Splendor

The praise courts where you experience the singing of angelic voices crying out Holy OH God Almighty. Like in the Bible, where Jesus mentions a word of thanks through praise and worship. Not to mention, every time I've gone to heaven, I have always heard music. The music was so pure and beautiful that it caught your attention. I thought if heaven's sound is praise, that explains why the enemy loves to attack music by lacing it with flesh that the people are receiving seeds of the flesh unknowingly until hours and days later when those seeds spring up. First, let me say I'm not coming against worldly music. However, what I am saying is to be careful. What's allowed in your ear gate can be the very hindrance that keeps you from going to your next level. I practice a rule while listening that has helped me. When I listen to anything, I always look for the sound of God. Yes, you heard me the sound of God. He has a sound that transcends everything that represents Him. Do you know the sound of God? If not then, it's time to learn, and if you do, it is time to take that sound deeper that the sound will penetrate every part of you, allowing the Lord's plans to be activated and set in motion.

ACTIVATION EXERCISE #1

Now let's activate our ears to hear not of this world using what some say is a prayer, but I say it's a prayer song using Psalm 23.

"The Lord, our shepherd that we shall not want. He makes me lie down in green pastures; he leadeth me beside the still waters. He restoreth my soul: he leadeth me in the paths of righteousness for his name's sake. Yea though I walk through the valley of the shadow of death, I will fear no evil; for thou art with me; thy rod and thy staff they comfort me. Thou preparest a table before me in the presence of mine enemies: thou anoint my head with oil; my cup runneth over. Surely goodness and mercy shall follow me all the days of my life: and I will dwell in the house of the Lord forever."

Can you hear the Lord your shepherd singing these things unto you? Can you hear the water as it stills? Can you hear His voice leading you unto the path of righteousness for His name's sake? Do you hear the voice of the enemy with fear and evil being driven out? For the rod and staff has come and banged on the ground removing your enemies. Do you hear dishes from God's table being set upon the table? Focus your mind, take a deep breath, and relax. Tell yourself we are before the King. Now, what do you hear? Can you hear the east wind blowing in the new for you? These are just the first steps.

ACTIVATION EXERCISE #2

Now let's go deeper into activations. Now sing these.

<u>Heavenly Praise Song #1(Revelation 4:8)</u>

Holy, holy - blessed is the Lord God Almighty; who was, and is and is to come!

Holy, holy - holy is the Lord God Almighty; who was, and is and is to come!

Holy, holy - holy is the Lord God Almighty; who was, and is and is to come!

Worthy, Worthy, worthy is the God Almighty; who was, and is to come!

Worthy, Worthy, worthy is the God Almighty; who was, and is to come!

Worthy, Worthy, worthy is the God Almighty; who was, and is to come!

Holy, Holy, Holy is the God Almighty; who was, and is to come!

Holy, Holy, Holy is the God Almighty; who was, and is to come!

Holy, Holy, Holy is the God Almighty; who was, and is to come!

<u>Heavenly Praise Song # 2 (Revelations 4:9)</u>

Glory and Honor is here
Glory and Honor is here
and thanks to him that sat on the throne

Who lives forever and ever!
Glory and Honor is here
Glory and Honor is here

and thanks to him that sat on the throne

Who lives forever and ever!
Glory and Honor is here
Glory and Honor is here
and thanks to him that sat on the throne
Who lives forever and ever!

Heavenly Praise Song # 3 (Revelations 4:10-11)

Worship him that liveth forever and ever
Casting down our crowns before the throne
We cry - Thou are worthy, O Lord
To receive Glory and honor and power
For thy pleasure, we were created.

Now that you have sung biblical songs that the Lord gave us in His Word, what do you hear? Did the Lord bless you with the music of expectation that will turn into sight to show you what is to come out of this activation process? Open your mind to hear Him differently than just in the small soft voice. That is only one way the Lord speaks. As the study continues in this book, we will discuss eight lessons on hearing the Lord and then activate what we learned with prophetic songs of activation.

There is no wrong or right way to sing these songs in this book. The only thing required is a clean heart and a desire to hear. Paul told us in 1 Corinthians 12:31 to eagerly desire the more significant gifts. Hearing the Lord is a more excellent gift. Why? It is greater because it's the beginning of knowing the

Lord in a greater capacity. Not just to hear and let what was said go in one ear and out the other but to obey, listen, and carry out what has been given. I have found that there are many in the body of Christ, and they have never heard the Lord. Then some hear but are unsure of whose voice they are hearing. That is a sign of an untended relationship. Think about people you spend time with naturally. You learn their communication patterns as well as dislikes and likes by spending time. If we fellowship with man to learn, then we must fellowship with the Lord at a great measure to understand who He is in every facet of His being.

We need to hear from the Lord that we will obtain the Kingdom's mysteries that we will be of significant effect when the Lord uses us. You can find a Scripture in Proverbs that tells us to get wisdom and then understanding. Wisdom is insight, and it opens the door of knowledge to carry out what you have learned. The more of the Kingdom we understand, the more wondrous works we can fulfill. Hearing from God is part of seeking the Lord. Isaiah 55:9 tells us that the heavens are higher than the earth, so are the ways of the Lord. Therefore, you can study God's Word, and the Lord can speak to you that way. You may worship, and the Lord may speak to you then. Or you can have vision and dreams, and the Lord can talk then. However, there is also the time you can hear the Lord's voice audibly. Sometimes His voice is soft, but then there are times when God's voice comes in like thunder. Psalm 29:3 states the voice of the LORD is upon the waters: the God of Glory thundereth: the LORD is upon many waters. If you continue to Psalm 29:4, the Bible adds the voice of the LORD is powerful; The voice

Introduction

of the LORD is full of majesty. To walk in power and glory at greater levels, we need to tap into hearing more than just from this world. God's voice is one primary access often overlooked. This book will demystify the voice of the Lord, not to make it familiar but that you will desire to communicate with the Lord every minute of the day.

According to Strong's Concordance, the Word for God's voice in Hebrew is Qolayah, and there are over five hundred and seven occurrences of the voice of the Lord in power with the Bible. This number is a clear sign the Lord is always trying to communicate with His people. However, His people are not in a position to speak with Him. The Lord wants you to hear His voice so that you will understand how He will destroy your enemies, just as He communicated in 1 Samuel 7:10. As the Philistines drew near to fight against Israel, Samuel was sacrificing the burnt offering. But that day, the LORD thundered against the Philistines and threw them into such confusion that they fled before Israel. He doesn't just want you to hear, but just as He spoke to the earth when formed. The Lord wants to talk to you that you will transform into what is placed within. He wants His people to know naturally and spiritually He has come on your behalf.

See, on that great day when the earth was formed, God's voice became law. Law that everything above, within, and under the world must obey what had been spoken from the Lord. We need that voice that everything follows to say unto His creation, which is us that everything in our lives will line up. We are the only thing created that has a choice to follow because of the free will of the Lord upon us. However, everything else must obey without choice. We need His spoken authority. According to Romans 10:17, so then faith comes by hearing and hearing by the Word of God. We need to listen to the Kingdom of God. That listening keeps us separated from this world that was more effective because we walk by faith and not by sight. Faith from on high that is cultivated by the Word of God and Kingdom worship. For we were created to worship and praise the Lord freely, this solidifies the sovereignty of God. Psalm 68:33 states to Him who rides upon the highest heavens of old; behold, His mighty voice resounds. The Lord's voice echoes throughout the world, but we must train our ears to not just focus on physical hearing but spiritually that we won't miss the reverberates of the Lord. The Lord's divine voice primary focus is to:

Strike Terror into Hearts of Sinners
Genesis 3:8

And they heard the voice of the LORD God walking in the garden in the cool of the day: and Adam and his wife hid themselves from the presence of the LORD God amongst the trees of the garden.

A Still Soft Voice
1 Kings 19:12

And after the earthquake a fire; but the LORD was not in the fire: and after the fire a still small voice.

Full of Majesty
Ezekiel 43:2

And, behold, the Glory of the God of Israel came from the way of the east: and his voice was like a noise of many waters: and the earth shined with his Glory.

Witnessing to Christ's Divinity
Matthew 17:5
While he was yet spake, behold, a bright cloud overshadowed them: and behold a voice out of the cloud, which said, This is my beloved Son, in whom I am well pleased; hear ye him.

Misunderstood by Men
John 12:28-29
Father, glorify thy name. Then came a voice from heaven, saying, I have both glorified it and will glorify it again. Therefore, the people that stood by and heard it said that it thundered: others said, An angel spake to him.

Know that you understand that God speaks and why you are ready to listen. He that has an ear let them hear what the Spirit of the Lord is saying.

INSTRUCTIONS

Now that you understand why it is essential to hear from the Lord. Here are some instructions. First, get a tablet or journal book that you can write. I know many rather have an electronic device; however, I recommend an old fashion journal that you can copy down all you hear. Once you have mastered the art of hearing, then you can graduate to an electronic device. Be sure to follow the lesson plan in this book. Read the lesson first and then meditate on the Scriptures given, pausing after everyone and being sure to digest them. Then go to the activation sections. Take your time and read each song and read the supporting Scriptures. Just as God tells us instructions are necessary, following these instructions is essential. For the Lord will respond to your obedience, for it was He who set the directions.

LESSON 1

Hear

WITHIN THIS LESSON, WE will focus on hearing. According to Webster's Dictionary, the term " hear " means to perceive, become aware of ear one, gain knowledge of hearing two, or understand hearing [3]. It also means law: to listen to legal arguments to give a legal hearing to [4a] or aw: to take testimony from [4b]. The definition doesn't just stop there; the word also, when used as an intransitive verb, means to have the capacity of perceiving sound: to be able to become aware of sound [1], to gain information: LEARN [2a], and to receive communication [2b].

You will find over thirty-two instances of the Word using this definition within the Bible. The first thing you need to understand, just like with any form of communication, you must be willing to listen. If you are fearful, this will block your hearing. It would help if you were not afraid to hear from your creator. He wants you to get to know Him better that you will get to know yourself more clearly. If there's fear, I come against all manner of fear that is not rooted in the reverential fear of the Lord. Any other fear is a hindrance, and it will work against your hearing. I also come against carnality. Wanting to hear the

Lord's voice for the wrong reasons will cause you to lose out on the most incredible access you will ever encounter; hearing directly from the Lord is a privilege. Do not be like Simon in Acts 8:18, who only wanted the spirit's gift for his selfish gain. The Lord doesn't respond to selfishness. For He was found selfless when He gave His life upon the cross for you and me. Therefore, I beckon you to surrender unto the Lord, casting down every idol in your heart and allowing the Lord to take His rightful place in your life (Psalms 51:10-19). Allowing the Lord to cleanse your heart and renew your spirit, opening up doors where you will never want to return.

Now that your heart has been cleaned, let us study the Scriptures that focus on hearing. It was a shocker to me while teaching when I heard people in leadership say they had never heard from God. Shocking because if you have never heard from Him, how do you know what direction He wants your ministry to go? Then there is God's perfect will; without hearing from God, how would you know if you're in His will? It's like when in a relationship. If the person you are in a relationship with never tells you their likes or dislikes for something, how can you know them? This example is carnal because the Lord is so much more, but my point is if you don't know Him, why would He show you the mysteries of His Kingdom? To know Him is to know Him. Know the things that you thought were out of reach or even impossible to obtain. Now let's pray for the desire of greater revelation within your relationship by hearing.

PRAYER

Dear Heavenly Father, we thank You for loving us enough to desire to speak with us. Lord, thank You for wanting us to know You in new and revealing ways. Lord, we ask You to create in us a clean heart and a right spirit that you will dwell with us in new ways. Lord, we ask for the full armor of the Lord that is in Ephesians 6:10-18 to be laced upon us that were protected from the principalities and rulers of darkness that will try to stop the communication. Lord, as You bind our armor, we ask You to open our ears to hear You like never before. We invite You to come against every spiritual plug or hindrance that would block Your voice. As we meditate on Your Scripture, You will take us to new streams and rivers that will listen to new plans for our lives that will shift us into the kings and queens You have called us to be for Your Kingdom. We ask all these things in your Son Jesus' name, amen.

Scriptures to Meditate on Hearing

1. Deuteronomy 31:12-13
    a. 12 Gather the people together, men and women, and children, and thy stranger that is within thy gates, that they may hear, and that they may learn, and fear the Lord your God and observe to do all the words of this law: And that their children, which have not known anything, may hear, and learn to fear the Lord your God, as long as ye live in the land whither ye go over Jordan to possess it.

2. 1 Kings 8:30
    a. And hearken thou to the supplication of thy servant, and thy people Israel, when they shall pray toward this place: and hear thou in heaven thy dwelling place: and when thou hearest, forgive.

3. 2 Chronicles 6:21
    a. Hearken therefore unto the supplications of thy servant, and thy people Israel, which they shall make toward this place: hear thou from thy dwelling place, even from heaven; and when thou hearest, forgive.

4. 1 Kings 18:26
    a. And they took the bullock which was given them, and they dressed it, and called on the name of Baal from morning even until noon, saying, O Baal, hear us. But there was no voice, nor any that answered. And they leaped upon the altar which was made.

5. Job 31:35
    a. Oh, that one would hear me! Behold, my desire is that the Almighty would answer me, and that mine adversary had written a book.

6. Psalm 4:1
    a. Hear me when I call, O God of my righteousness: thou hast enlarged me when I was in distress; have mercy upon me and hear my prayer.

7. Psalm 39:12
   a. Hear my prayer, O Lord, and give ear unto my cry; hold not thy peace at my tears: for I am a stranger with thee, and a sojourner, as all my fathers were.

8. Psalm 54:2
   a. Hear my prayer, O God; give ear to the words of my mouth.

9. Psalm 84:8
   a. O Lord God of hosts, hear my prayer: give ear, O God of Jacob. Selah.

10. Psalm 102:1
    a. Hear my prayer, O Lord, and let my cry come unto thee.

11. Psalm 143:1
    a. Hear my prayer, O Lord, give ear to my supplications: in thy faithfulness answer me and in thy righteousness.

12. Psalm 51:8
    a. Make me hear joy and gladness; that the bones which thou hast broken may rejoice.

13. Psalm 59:7
    a. Behold, they belch out with their mouth: swords are in their lips: for who, say they, doth hear?

14. Psalm 85:8
    a. I will hear what God the Lord will speak: for he will speak peace unto his people, and to his saints: but let them not turn again to folly.

15. Psalm 94:9
    a. He that planted the ear, shall he not hear? He that formed the eye, shall he not see?

16. Proverb 22:17
    a. Bow down thine ear, and hear the words of the wise, and apply thine heart unto my knowledge.

17. Ecclesiastes 5:1
    a. Keep thy foot when thou goest to the house of God and be more ready to hear than to give the sacrifice of fools: for they consider not that they do evil.

18. Isaiah 1:2
    a. Hear, O heavens, and give ear, O earth: for the Lord hath spoken, I have nourished and brought up children, and they have rebelled against me.

19. Mark 4:12
    a. That seeing they may see, and not perceive, and hearing they may hear, and not understand; lest at any time they should be converted, and their sins should be forgiven them.

Hear

20. Isaiah 33:13
    a. Hear, ye that are far off, what I have done; and, ye that are near, acknowledge my might.

21. Isaiah 34:1
    a. Come near, ye nations, to hear; and hearken ye people: let the earth hear, and all that is therein; the world, and all things that come forth of it.

22. Isaiah 55:3
    a. Incline your ear, and come unto me: hear, and your soul shall live; and I will make an everlasting covenant with you, even the sure mercies of David.

23. Isaiah 65:24
    a. And it shall come to pass, that before they call, I will answer; and while they are yet speaking, I will hear.

24. Ezekiel 3:27
    a. But when I speak with thee, I will open thy mouth, and thou shalt say unto them, Thus saith the Lord God; He that heareth, let him hear; and he that forbeareth, let him forbear: for they are a rebellious house.

25. Acts 28:26
    a. Saying, Go unto this people, and say, Hearing ye shall hear, and shall not understand; and seeing ye shall see, and not perceive:

26. Luke 10:24
    a. For I tell you, that many prophets and kings have desired to see those things which ye see, and have not seen them; and to hear those things which ye hear, and have not heard them.

27. Matthew 18:16
    a. But if he will not hear thee, then take with thee one or two more, that in the mouth of two or three witnesses every word may be established.

28. Mark 4:24
    a. And he said unto them, Take heed what ye hear: with what measure ye mete, it shall be measured to you: and unto you that hear shall more be given.

29. Luke 8:18
    a. Take heed therefore how ye hear: for whosoever hath, to him shall be given; and whosoever hath not, from him shall be taken even that which he seemeth to have.

30. Luke 16:31
    a. And he said unto him, If they hear not Moses and the prophets, neither will they be persuaded, though one rose from the dead.

31. John 5:25
    a. Verily, verily, I say unto you, The hour is coming, and now is, when the dead shall hear the voice of the Son of God: and they that hear shall live.

32. John 12:47
    a. And if any man hear my words, and believe not, I judge him not: for I came not to judge the world, but to save the world.

33. Acts 3:22
    a. For Moses truly said unto the fathers, A prophet shall the Lord your God raise up unto you of your brethren, like unto me; him shall ye hear in all things whatsoever he shall say unto you.

34. Acts 7:37
    a. This is that Moses, which said unto the children of Israel, A prophet shall the Lord your God raise up unto you of your brethren, like unto me; him shall ye hear.

35. Romans 10:14
    a. How then shall they call on him in whom they have not believed? and how shall they believe in him of whom they have not heard? and how shall they hear without a preacher?

36. James 1:19
    a. Wherefore, my beloved brethren, let every man be swift to hear, slow to speak, slow to wrath.

ACTIVATIONS

Activation Song One
Spirit of the Lord Fill this Room

Spirit of Glory & the Spirit of Power
Come and take your place
Spirit of Glory & the Spirit of Power
Come and take your place
Spirit of Glory
Spirit of Power
Come on in this room
Holy Spirit, we need You
We need You
We need you in this room
Come and Take Your Place
Spirit of the Lord fill this room
Spirit of The Lord fill this room
Come and take your place
We need You
We need You
Come and take your place.

SCRIPTURE SUPPORT

Divine Presence
Psalms 16:11
Thou wilt shew me the path of Life: in thy presence is fullness of joy; at thy right hand there are pleasures for evermore.

Christ Presence
John 12:26

If any man serves me, let him follow me; and where I am, there shall also my servant be: if any man serves me, he will my Father honour.

WORSHIP EXPRESSION

This song invokes our right to be in the Lord's divine presence. We must use our greatest weapon, our mouth, to activate our request and invite the presence of God to come and meet us in worship, praise, or even serve Him by ministering to the people. We must put a demand on Him, reminding Him of our desires that He will come and all that are present lives will be changed.

SELF-EVALUATION

1. What did the song invoke in you?
2. Did you feel the presence of God entering the room?
3. Once He entered, what did you receive?

PRAYER

Dear Heavenly Father, the Creator of all things, we thank You for the prophetic song of praise and worship. Lord, fill every place we dwell, including our persons, with Your presence like never before. Lord, overfill us until we overflow in You. Lord, cleanse our cups; if we have murky water that Your purification will come upon us that we can feel Your presence. Lord, help us to walk in Your Spirit like never before that we will hear the music of heaven, in Jesus' Holy name, Amen.

REFLECTION:

Hear

EARS TO PROCLAIM GOD'S SPLENDOR

AFFIRMATION:

Acts 7:55

But he, being full of the Holy Ghost, looked up steadfastly, into heavens, and saw the Glory of God and Jesus standing on the right hand of God.

Hear

PROCLAMATIONS:

Acts 7:56

And said, Behold, I see the heavens opened and the Son of man standing on the right hand of God.

Activation: Song Two
We Need You Today

Jesus - Jesus
We need you today
What we need is you
To enter in this room
What we need is you today

Jesus Jesus
We need you today
To be in the room
Let you Glory rest
Let your Glory rest
Today

For the Father will only come
If you are here
Jesus enter this room
Today

Father make this place holy
Send down your Glory

SCRIPTURE SUPPORT

Purification
2 Corinthians 7:1

Therefore, since we have these promises, dear friends, let us purify ourselves from everything that contaminates body and spirit, perfecting holiness out of reverence for God.

Calling
1 Peter 1:15-16
But just as he who called you is holy, so be holy in all you do; for it is written: "Be holy, because I am holy."

Peace
Hebrews 12:14
Make every effort to live in peace with everyone and to be holy; without holiness no one will see the Lord.

WORSHIP EXPRESSION

This song began to flow from my heart one day as I was in prayer. I had been asking the Lord for help, and for Him to show me how to usher in His presence greater for the people. I've learned that nothing is accomplished by ourselves, and to see signs and wonders, we must invite the Lord in the room. Not just Him alone but also His Son because we can't get nowhere without His Son, Jesus. The fact that Jesus has opened the door that we can even communion with the Father. However, many only see half of the power because they invite one part of God and not the other. I have learned to see all of Him, and we must want to see all of Him. For just like He takes a married couple who were two and makes them one. The great I AM (Exodus 3:14), who is the Father, sent His Son (John 3:16) to marry His people (2 Corinthians 11:2), and the Son as a gift to His bride sent the Holy Spirit (John 14:26). All three make one. Just like you can't leave a husband or a wife out of a marriage and call it a marriage. You can not leave out all the facets of God if you want to see every measure of Him show up in your life.

As the Word says, no one comes before the Father unless through the Son. The SON gives access, so call on Him. Ask Him into the place you dwell and watch everything around you change. Brokenness, confusion, lack, unforgiveness, and even the old you will be gone, and your authentic identity will be found. Why? Because, Jesus holds your identity.

Purification starts by inviting the Lord into your life.

SELF-EVALUATION

1. Did you invite Christ into your place of dwelling?
2. Did you make your portions?
3. Once he entered, what did you receive?

PRAYER

Dear Heavenly Father, the ruler of all things, we thank You for sending Your Son to die for us. Lord unlock our callings from with us drawing a peace that surpasses all understanding. Helping us to understand who we are and whom we belong to. Allow the song of identity to full us beyond what has been shown in Jesus' Holy Name, Amen.

Hear

REFLECTION:

Ears to Proclaim God's Splendor

Hear

AFFIRMATION:

2 Timothy 1:9 (NIV)

He has saved us and called us to a holy life—not because of anything we have done but because of his own purpose and grace. This grace was given us in Christ Jesus before the beginning of time.

Ears to Proclaim God's Splendor

PROCLAMATIONS:

Psalms 119:9 (NIV)

How can a young person stay on the path of purity? By living according to your Word.

Activation: Song Three
Prince of Peace

Hallelujah Alleluia
Lord we bless
We bless Your Name
We lift you high above the heavens
We bless your name
For you are worthy of the praise
We bless your name

Hallelujah Alleluia
Lord we bless
Hallelujah Alleluia
Lord, we bless Your Holy Name
Prince of Peace
Bread of Life

You're the lover of my soul
My soul
We just bless your name
For your worthy to be praise
We say
Hallelujah Alleluia
Lord we bless
Hallelujah Alleluia
Lord, We bless Your Holy Name

Ears to Proclaim God's Splendor

SCRIPTURE SUPPORT

Prince of Peace

Isaiah 9:6

For unto us a child is born, unto us a son is given: and the government shall be upon his shoulder: and his name shall be called Wonderful, Counselor, The mighty God, The everlasting Father, The Prince of Peace.

Bread of Life

John 6:35

And Jesus said to them, "I am the bread of Life. He who comes to Me shall never hunger, and he who believes in Me shall never thirst.

John 6:48

I am the bread of Life.

Lover of Our Soul.

Psalms 40:2

He brought me up also out of a horrible pit, out of the miry clay, and set my feet upon a rock and established my goings

WORSHIP EXPRESSION

There will be a time when you will feel the love of God come upon you. There is no real word to describe everything He does for us. This song was birthed out of me while worshipping and expressing the love for God. Sometimes it is not what He is to you naturally but who He is to you ultimately. The Lord has done more for me than I could ever do for myself. Most of what He does I don't deserve. I often worship God because when I was ready to die, He came and saved me while I was yet a sinner fornicating, lying, murderous, envious, and a rebellious filthy mess. He came when I was ready to give up and kill myself because I lacked earthy love and acceptance and suffered repeated rejection. He came and counted me worthy of life, and He didn't just give me life, but it more abundantly. This song is a constant reminder of the abundant life.

SELF-EVALUATION

1. Have you ever felt the loving power of God?
2. If not, have you acknowledged Him as your Lord and Savior?
3. If no, then start with acceptance. Read and follow the direction of Romans 10:9.
4. If you have accepted the Lord Jesus as your Lord and Savior, then ask Him to come that you may experience His touch.
5. If you had felt the loving power of God before, when was the last time? Ask Him to come now as you are reading.

PRAYER

Dear Heavenly Father, the lover of our souls. The God that loves us beyond anything on this earth. Lord, we come to You asking to be cleansed from anything that is hindering us from experiencing You in greater depths. Help us accept the divine plan You have for us and not walk in unbelief, which makes anything we do for You insufficient. Lord, help us to trust your work and to walk in greater faith, allowing us to become zealous about the things concerning You. We desire to walk in the first fruit of holiness being sufficient for Your work. Lord, fall on us that we may experience You in a new way. Allow us to see You never like before in our lives. Take us to new heights and depths beyond anything we could have ever imagined. Lord, help us be like your Son, Christ, that we would love what You love and hate what You hate, all while carrying out the vocation You have before us. For many are called, but few chosen. Lord, allow us to pick You, and as we draw unto You, then you will draw unto us, causing our faith to increase as we hear Your word. We ask all these things in your Son Jesus' Holy name, Amen.

REFLECTION:

_____

_____

_____

_____

_____

_____

_____

_____

Hear

Ears to Proclaim God's Splendor

AFFIRMATION:

Romans 12:12

Rejoicing in hope; patient in tribulation; continuing instant in prayer.

PROCLAMATIONS:

Romans 14:8

For whether we live, we live unto the Lord; and whether we die, we die unto the Lord; whether we live therefore, or die, we are the Lord's.

Activation: Song Four
Praise Your Name

I feel your presence
I feel your Glory
What I want to do is
Praise your Name

I feel your presence
I feel your Glory
What I want to do is
Praise your Name

I feel your presence
I feel your Glory
What I want to do is
Praise your Name

Praise your name
For Lord we
Praise you
Praise you - Oh, Lord
We feel your presence
We feel your Glory
What we want to do is praise your Name

SCRIPTURE SUPPORT

Presence of God
Psalms 16:11

Thou wilt shew me the path of Life: in thy presence is fullness of joy; at they right hand there are pleasures for evermore.

Living In Christ
Acts 17:28 (NASB 1995)
For in Him we live and move and exist, as we even some of your own poets have said, 'For we also are His Children.'

God's Hand
Job 12:10 (HCSB)
The Life of every living thing is in His hand, as well as the breath of all mankind.

WORSHIP EXPRESSION

Have you ever been minding your own business and all of a sudden, you feel the presence of God? You get chill bumps, or the hair on your neck stands up. Or you may experience His fire, winds, or touch. Whichever category you may find yourself in, God has a way of letting His people know He is a living God. He is not sitting as a display, but He moves throughout the Earth, seeing His people and inviting others to become His people. His love never stops nor fails. I love to have experiences like this because I know there is an assurance that God loves me and that I'm one of His own. Not to say but to honestly know and believe it. I have decided to live within the presence of God. Simultaneously, moving according to His will and being as He has called me to be. This song reminded me of that. Not just to feel the Lord's presence but to become a part of the reality.

SELF-EVALUATION

1. What did the song invoke in you?
2. Did you feel the presence of God enter the room as you sang the song?
3. Once God entered the room, what did you receive? If He didn't enter, sing the song again. Close your eyes. Relax and allow your ears to hear.

PRAYER

Dear Heavenly Father, the originator of all things, we thank you for the prophetic song of admiration and reverence. Lord, fill every place we dwell, including individuals, with Your presence like never before. Lord fill us until we overflow in you. Lord, cleanse our cups; if we have murky water, may Your purification come upon us that we can feel Your presence. Lord, help us to walk in Your Spirit like never before that we will hear the music of Heaven. Lord, send Your divine help and support that we may be preserved while doing Your work. That our bodies will age gracefully and the wear of life will not take us before our time, in Jesus' Holy name, Amen.

REFLECTION:

_____

_____

_____

Hear

Ears to Proclaim God's Splendor

AFFIRMATION:

Psalm 139:7 (NIV)

Where can I go for Your Spirit? Or where can I flee from Your presence?

PROCLAMATIONS:

Jeremiah 29:13 (BSB)
You will seek Me and find Me when you search for Me with all your heart.

Activation: Song Five
Worthy Praise

Glory to His name
Let us shout and praise
He is worthy to be praise
He is worthy to be praise
Praise His Name!

Jesus is His name
Let us give Him praise
For he is worthy to be praise
Worthy to be praise
Let us praise

Glory to His name
Let us shout and praise
He is worthy to be praise
He is worthy to be praise
Praise His Name!

Jesus is His name
Let us give Him praise
For he is worthy to be praised
Worthy to be praised
Let us praise

SCRIPTURE SUPPORT

The glory of the Lord
John 1:14 (NKJV)

And the Word became flesh, and dwelt among us, and we saw His Glory, Glory as of the only begotten from the Father, full of grace and truth.

The Lord is Worthy
Revelation 4:11 (ESV)

"Worthy are You, our Lord and our God, to receive glory and honor and power; for You created all things, and because of Your will they existed and were created."

WORSHIP EXPRESSION

To truly worship the Lord, we must walk in great humility. Understanding no matter how much we accomplish on this earth, it all comes from the source, which is our Lord and Savior Christ. There are times even ministers need to remember that our Lord and Savior Christ is working healing, deliverance, or guiding our introducing Christ unto people. The Lord enables you to achieve those things and not yourself. Therefore, no need to get proud of any work in God's Kingdom that you have accomplished because it was the Lord's accomplishment. We're merely vessels used but can be replaced by another selected in an instant. I learned to stay low before the people but high in God. That saying keeps me grounded and humbled, reminding me that those called to the front of the line should serve the people the greatest. The world does it backward by saying those on top deserve more that is not God's way. He takes the last and makes them first. He takes the one with the low head and lifts it.

When walking in any form of arrogance, we understand and know there is a great fall ahead. It is just a matter of time. I found that no matter what the financial status of people, they can walk in pride. Our greatest destroyers are the lust of the flesh and eyes and the pride of life. Yes, lust is what the Word calls it because it draws you out and perverts, making anything that touches it unclean.

On the other hand, pride affects everything you see, feel, and accomplish. Lust and pride will contaminate everything exposed unto it. Thus, I chose to fear the Lord and not break any commandments and to worship Him, which keeps the enemy away from me because he can't stand praises except unto himself. Things may happen, but as long as I keep my posture focused on God and not on people, places, and things, I can complete what the Lord ordained for me before I ever was placed in my mother's womb.

SELF-EVALUATION

1. Do you have a reverent fear of the Lord?
2. What does it mean to you to glorify the Lord?
3. What is your favorite expression to demonstrate your love for God?

PRAYER

Hear

Dear Heavenly Father, the source of all things, Oh, how worthy you are, Lord. If I had a thousand tongues, I couldn't praise You enough. If You find anything not pleasing within me, Lord, please take it out. Lord, deliver me from any sources of pride. If I have the lust of the flesh, the lust of the eyes, or pride of life, Lord deliver me today that I may carry out Your will for my life and serve those called unto me as Christ did, in Jesus' Holy name, Amen.

REFLECTION:

Ears to Proclaim God's Splendor

AFFIRMATION:

2 Corinthians 4:6 (NASB)

For God, who said, "Light shall shine out of darkness,' is the One who has shone in our hearts to give the Light of the knowledge of the glory of God in the face of Christ.

EARS TO PROCLAIM GOD'S SPLENDOR

PROCLAMATIONS:

Psalm 145:5 (NASB)

On the glorious splendor of Your majesty And on Your wonderful works, I will meditate.

LESSON 2

Heard

*N*OW THAT YOU HAVE grasped the concept of hearing. Let us move to the art of being heard. The word heard is past tense (or past participle) for hear. Heard means to perceive with the ear the sound made by (someone or something) [1] or be told or informed of. [2] In Lesson one, we focused on hearing now let examine what you heard. We know that there is a devil, and he is always trying to interfere with what God is doing. Therefore we must have checks and balances to ensure what we heard came from God. One way to verify is to determine if what we heard aligns with the Word of God. Here is a question to ask yourself, does what you received bring glory unto God? If the response is yes, then you can compare what you heard to the Word of God. If no, toss it out. Remember, everything even correction brings glory unto the Father.

1 Corinthians 1:31 states in KJV, "That, according as it is written, He that glorieth, let him glory in the Lord." I also like what the American Standard Bible says about the verse, which is "so that, just as it is written, "LET HIM WHO BOASTS, BOAST IN THE LORD." Therefore, I advise you if while looking up

the Bible's answer, and it isn't found, wait to receive what you heard in your heart. It may not be from the Lord. You will need to be careful with this; many of us are not well studied in the Word and can misinterpret what the Lord is saying. So a good practice is to have two journal books. One for what you found in the Bible and things you are still searching out. Sometimes in spending time with the Lord, He will give you clarity of something you heard, and it will help you understand the principle of what the Lord is trying to communicate next if you asked a question and got no response.

What type of problem did you ask about? Was the question directly to the point, or was it open-ended? Remember, you are dealing with God thus we do not have conversation with Him in the same manner like you do with human beings. Remember early on, I told you what our brother Isaiah taught us in chapter 55. The Lord ways are higher. He doesn't have a conversation to take. Every word given is out of purpose. Therefore you need to govern yourself accordingly to get answers from the Lord. Be direct, ask the question in a yes and no manner and be patient. Remember, you are learning how you and God communicate. If you're one who has already established communication, maybe you should try a new form of contact. As discussed in this book, ask the Lord to talk in songs.

Another standard error in communicating with the Father is doing all the talking and allowing your flesh to give you answers. Remember, be anxious for nothing; the Lord will answer His question within His time and His way. I have found sometimes He answers right away; and sometimes it takes time, but

I know He wants to answer, but you must be patient. Being patient means: don't ramble on and on like most of us do when we talk. It is human nature to wander without purpose; remember, you are not talking in a low estate but a high place where the glory dwells, thus follow the sending and receiving taught in basic methods of communication.

BASIC COMMUNICATION METHODS

Adler and Towne describe communication as a process between at least two people that begins when one person wants to communicate. Communication originates as mental images within a person who desires to convey those images to another. Mental images can include ideas, thoughts, pictures, and emotions. The person who wants to communicate is called the sender. To transfer an image to another person, the sender first must transpose or translate the pictures into symbols that receivers can understand. Symbols often are words but can be pictures, sounds, or our sense of information (touch or smell). Only through symbols can the mental images of a sender have meaning for others. The process of translating images into symbols is called encoding. This process is the basis of communication. Therefore if you are searching just for a word, you can use a vital image or sound that the Lord is trying to communicate to you and that is just as important as words. Remember, when decoding a message received that the earth is the Lords and the fullness thereof; thus, he can use every aspect of the earth to relate his message unto you.

SCRIPTURES TO MEDITATE ON BEING HEARD:

Ears to Proclaim God's Splendor

1. Genesis 3:8
   a. And they heard the voice of the Lord God walking in the garden in the cool of the day: and Adam and his wife hid themselves from the presence of the Lord God amongst the trees of the garden.

2. Exodus 3:7
   a. And the Lord said, I have surely seen the affliction of my people which are in Egypt, and have heard their cry by reason of their taskmasters; for I know their sorrows;

3. Deuteronomy 4:12
   a. And the Lord spake unto you out of the midst of the fire: ye heard the voice of the words, but saw no similitude; only ye heard a voice.

4. Job 4:16
   a. It stood still, but I could not discern the form thereof: an image was before mine eyes, there was silence, and I heard a voice, saying,

5. Psalm 48:8
   a. As we have heard, so have we seen in the city of the Lord of hosts, in the city of our God: God will establish it forever. Selah.

6. Psalm 66:19

Heard

    a. But verily God hath heard me; he hath attended to the voice of my prayer.

7. Psalm 116:1
   a. I love the Lord, because he hath heard my voice and my supplications.

8. Psalm 118:21
   a. I will praise thee: for thou hast heard me, and art become my salvation.

9. Ecclesiastes 9:16-17
   a. Then said I, Wisdom is better than strength: nevertheless, the poor man's wisdom is despised, and his words are not heard.
   b. The words of wise men are heard in quiet more than the cry of him that ruleth among fools.

10. Isaiah 40:21
    a. Have ye not known? have ye not heard? hath it not been told you from the beginning? have ye not understood from the foundations of the earth?

11. Isaiah 64:4
    a. For since the beginning of the world men have not heard, nor perceived by the ear, neither hath the eye seen, O God, beside thee, what he hath prepared for him that waiteth for him.

12. Isaiah 66:8

a. Who hath heard such a thing? who hath seen such things? Shall the earth be made to bring forth in one day? or shall a nation be born at once? for as soon as Zion travailed, she brought forth her children.

13. Jeremiah 8:6
    a. I hearkened and heard, but they spake not aright: no man repented him of his wickedness, saying, What have I done? every one turned to his course, as the horse rusheth into the battle.

14. Jeremiah 31:18
    a. I have surely heard Ephraim bemoaning himself thus; Thou hast chastised me, and I was chastised, as a bullock unaccustomed to the yoke: turn thou me, and I shall be turned; for thou art the Lord my God.

15. Daniel 12:8
    a. And I heard, but I understood not: then said I, O my Lord, what shall be the end of these things?

16. Jonah 2:2
    a. And said, I cried by reason of mine affliction unto the Lord, and he heard me; out of the belly of hell cried I, and thou heardest my voice.

17. Malachi 3:16
    a. Then they that feared the Lord spake often one to another: and the Lord hearkened, and heard it, and a book of remembrance was written before him for

them that feared the Lord, and that thought upon his name.

18. Matthew 6:7
    a. But when ye pray, use not vain repetitions, as the heathen do: for they think that they shall be heard for their much speaking.

19. John 11:41
    a. Then they took away the stone from the place where the dead was laid. And Jesus lifted up his eyes, and said, Father, I thank thee that thou hast heard me.

20. Acts 4:4
    a. Howbeit many of them which heard the word believed; and the number of the men was about five thousand.

21. Acts 4:20
    a. For we cannot but speak the things which we have seen and heard.

22. Romans 10:18
    a. But I say, Have they not heard? Yes verily, their sound went into all the earth, and their words unto the ends of the world.

23. 2 Corinthians 12:4
    a. How that he was caught up into paradise, and heard unspeakable words, which it is not lawful for a man to utter.

24. Philippians 4:9
    a. Those things, which ye have both learned, and received, and heard, and seen in me, do: and the God of peace shall be with you.

25. 2 Timothy 2:2
    a. And the things that thou hast heard of me among many witnesses, the same commit thou to faithful men, who shall be able to teach others also.

26. Hebrews 2:1
    a. Therefore we ought to give the more earnest heed to the things which we have heard, lest at any time we should let them slip.

27. Hebrews 4:2
    a. For unto us was the gospel preached, as well as unto them: but the word preached did not profit them, not being mixed with faith in them that heard it.

28. Hebrews 5:7
    a. Who in the days of his flesh, when he had offered up prayers and supplications with strong crying and tears unto him that was able to save him from death, and was heard in that he feared;

29. Hebrews 12:19
    a. And the sound of a trumpet, and the voice of words; which voice they that heard intreated that the word should not be spoken to them any more:

30. 1 John 1:1
    a. That which was from the beginning, which we have heard, which we have seen with our eyes, which we have looked upon, and our hands have handled, of the Word of life;

31. 1 John 1:3
    a. That which we have seen and heard declare we unto you, that ye also may have fellowship with us: and truly our fellowship is with the Father, and with his Son Jesus Christ.

32. 1 John 1:5
    a. This then is the message which we have heard of him, and declare unto you, that God is light, and in him is no darkness at all.

Activations: Song Six
Righteous One

Bless it Be the Name of The Lord
The Righteous One
The Righteous One

Bless it Be the Name of The Lord

Bless it Be the Name of The Lord
OH Righteous One
Righteous One

Bless it Be the Name of The Lord
The Righteous One
The Righteous One

Bless it Be the Name of The Lord
Bless it Be the Name of The Lord
OH Righteous One
Righteous One

SCRIPTURE SUPPORT

Righteous
1 John 2:1

My little children, these things write I unto you, that ye sin not. And if any man sin, we have an advocate with the Father, Jesus Christ the righteous:

Name of the Lord
1 Timothy 2:5

For there is one God and one mediator between God and men, the man Christ Jesus,

WORSHIP EXPRESSION

This song came at a time when I needed to be reminded who the Lord was in my life. Hardship can cause us to forget our righteous King. Hardship can cause us to drift backward. However, we must hold on, for the Lord is with us and He will protect us. He will keep us in peace while we go through. Don't you dare give up and don't you dare quit. For our King the righteous one sitting on the throne will never leave nor forsake you.

SELF-EVALUATION

1. Do you believe the Lord will never leave nor forsake you?
2. Can you feel the comfort of the Lord?
3. What has the Lord revealed about the purpose of his comfort unto you?

PRAYER

Dear Heavenly Father, the originator of all things, we thank you for the prophetic song of comfort and truth. Lord, fill every place we dwell, including individuals, with your presence like never before. Lord fill us until You consume us. Lord, help us to walk in your Spirit like never before that we will hear the music of Heaven. Lord, send Your divine help and support that we may be preserved while doing Your work. That our bodies will age gracefully and he wear of life will not take us before our time, in Jesus Holy name, Amen.

Ears to Proclaim God's Splendor

REFLECTION:

Heard

Ears to Proclaim God's Splendor

AFFIRMATION:

John 14:16 (BSB)

And I will ask the Father, and He will give you another Advocate to be with you forever.

Heard

PROCLAMATIONS:

3 John 1:4 (NIV)
I have no greater joy than to hear that my children are walking in the truth.

Activations: Song Seven
I Need More

More
More
More
I need More

More of Your Power
More of Your Grace
More of Your Spirit
Take your place, Lord

More
More
More
I need More

More
More
More
Jesus, I need More

SCRIPTURE SUPPORT

Thirsty
Psalms 16:11
Thou wilt shew me the path of life: in thy presence is fullness of joy; at they right hand there are pleasures for evermore.

Living In Christ
Acts 17:28 (NASB 1995)
For in Him we live and move and exist, as we even some of your own poets have said, 'For we also are His Children.'

WORSHIP EXPRESSION

When I'm teaching or praying, the Lord will bring unto me a song. As you will see within this book, the Lord uses music to guide me as I carry out my assignment. He tells me when to praise Him, when to pray or when to release prophetic words. When the people were hungry for more, the Lord had me sing prophetically, requesting for more glory to hit the broadcast. The more I sang, the more God moved. That was one of my first times paying attention to more than the Lord's arrival but also how He came into the room. That is also when He gave me the great revelation of our relationship. He took me back to times of suffering and revealed how He would pour His melody upon me, which would cause the garment of praise to come. Once the garment came upon me, things would begin to break forth to a new day. The song variation would depend on what needed to take place within my life. The Lord had used music all the years, but I missed what He was doing because I was not sharpen in the prophetic. Now when I'm doing anything, I'm sure to listen for my instruction because I know when the music comes, the Lord will be in the mist.

SELF-EVALUATION

Ears to Proclaim God's Splendor

1. What avenue does the Lord use when He communicates with you?
2. How did the Lord communicate with you during this teaching?
3. What other ways do you desire for the Lord to communicate with you?

PRAYER

Dear Heavenly Father, the designer of all things, we thank You for the avenue of guidance and communication You use to direct us. Lord, help us to find every route of transmission You use to speak. Please help us to have the faith to hear that we will see. Teach us, Lord, great and wonderful things that will help move the body of Christ closer to You, in Jesus' Holy name, Amen.

REFLECTION:

_____
_____
_____
_____
_____
_____
_____

Heard

EARS TO PROCLAIM GOD'S SPLENDOR

AFFIRMATION:

Job 12:10

In whose hand is the soul of every living thing and the breath of all mankind.

PROCLAMATIONS:

Psalm 36:9

For with thee is the fountain of life: in thy light shall we see light.

Activations: Song Eight
You Tried It!

You Tried It
You Tried It
You Tried It
Aye
But You not Going to Win

You Tried It
You Tried It
Devil
But You not Gone to Win

You Tried It!
You Tried It
You Tried It
You Tried It
Aye
But You not Going to Win
You Tried It
You Tried It
Devil
But You not Gone to Win

SCRIPTURE SUPPORT

Victory
1 John 5:4

For whatsoever is born of God overcometh the world: and this is the victory that overcometh the world, even our faith.

Strength
Ephesians 6:10
Finally, my brethren, be strong in the Lord, and in the power of his might.

Deliverance & Blessing
Psalm 3:8
Salvation belongeth unto the Lord: thy blessing is upon thy people. Selah.

WORSHIP EXPRESSION

There are times when you're just tired. The enemy will try to block your hearing because he understands the more you hear from the throne of God, the less you are influenced by him. Why? It is because you are not living according to this world but in a world where his access has been denied. However, you must resist all of his tactics, take every word to the Bible, and take counsel with those found in righteousness. For the Word of God says there is safety in counsel. The counsel of men and angels. Remember, the Lord gives them to charge over us and can send information via angels. Also, remember in the Bible, there are numerous accounts of information provided via angels. Therefore do not discount communication from on high, for you were created a little lower than them, which allows angels to go before the throne. Don't be like our brother Zechariah discussed in Luke 1 and get a message from the angels but not receive the news; thus, being struck mute. However, in your case, your hearing access from heaven can be shut off for some time. Instead, try the spirit by the spirit by asking the voice to recognize our King as Lord and Savior. Remember, the devil is prideful and will never speak with a clear tongue that Jesus is Lord. Our fellow brothers, the angels, are another avenue for us to receive messages; however, our ears must be open to hearing that we may carry out what we heard. Daniel chapter ten is an excellent example of this when messenger angels came to confirm his prayer and deliver him greater revelation on what he was seeking.

SELF-EVALUATION

1. Did you feel the strength and victory as you sang the song?
2. What have you heard from the Lord concerning the topic?
3. Are you ready to receive messages from our fellow servants, the angels?

PRAYER

Dear Heavenly Father, the designer of all, we thank You for the prophetic song of confidence. We thank You for the strength You have deposited within, pouring the joy of the Lord upon us. Lord, stabilize our mind that we may be able to receive angelic visitations. Give us the words to say that will ensure who we are entertaining, for we know the devil loves to deceive by masking as an angel of light. However, let us see beyond his appearance and see the heart of the matter in which he comes, which will, in turn, give us continued victory over him over and over again. Lord, cleanse our ears to every message we have received that is not of You that we may be able to receive your seeds of destiny. Lord, we thank you for the strength you are imparting into us to not just hear but to carry out the things you have called unto us. We ask all these things in your Son Jesus' Holy name, Amen.

REFLECTION:

_____

_____

_____

_____

_____

_____

_____

_____

_____

_____

_____

_____

Ears to Proclaim God's Splendor

AFFIRMATION:

Micah 3:8

But truly I am full of power by the spirit of the Lord, and of judgment, and of might, to declare unto Jacob his transgression, and to Israel his sin.

Ears to Proclaim God's Splendor

PROCLAMATIONS:

Zechariah 4:6

Then he answered and spake unto me, saying, This is the word of the Lord unto Zerubbabel, saying, Not by might, nor by power, but by my spirit, saith the Lord of hosts.

Activations: Song Nine
This is How

This is how I Fight
This how is how I War
This is how I Fight
This how is how I War

Fight - Fight - Fight
War – War – War

This is how
This is how

This is how I Fight
This how is how I Win
This is how I Fight
This how is how I Win
Fight - Fight - Fight
Win – Win - Win

This is how
This is how
I fight with the Word
I fight with His grace
Fight by slapping the devil in his face

This is how
This is how
Aye

This is how
This is how
I praise my God all over the Place

This is how
This is how
This is how

So fight and war
Fight and War
Fight -Fight -Fight
War – War- War
Win – Win – Win

SCRIPTURE SUPPORT

Armor
Ephesians 6:11
Put on the whole armour of God, that ye may be able to stand against the wiles of the devil.

Fight
Matthew 24:6
And ye shall hear of wars and rumours of wars: see that ye be not troubled: for all these things must come to pass, but the end is not yet.

War
1 Timothy 6:12

Fight the good fight of faith, lay hold on eternal life, whereunto thou art also called, and hast professed a good profession before many witnesses.

WORSHIP EXPRESSION

This song came to me during a time of war. It seemed like every week, a new war was breaking out. There was war in my home, marriage, on my job, and within my ministry. All hell had broken loose, and I had no clue why or what to do. I began to cry and worship, asking the Lord what was going on because I complied with all He had ordered. In my immature stage, most times, when war comes, it comes because of disobedience, and the enemy buys up the opportunity to attack. However, this was not one of those times. This was a Job moment; I was tried for my faith. When the Lord tells the enemy have you tried my servant - type of moment. How do I know what kind of time it was? The Lord told me. Yes, you heard me, He said it to me because I asked. The Lord told me His grace was sufficient for my suffering, but then He sent that song unto me. As I sang the song, I could feel comfort and the weighty glory of the Lord. He was reminding me that even in war, the Lord is present. Just as in Revelations 4, we worship, this gains the Lord's attention and causes Him to sit on His throne. In this place, He is ready to dispatch your help that you will prevail against every enemy that arises against you. Thus, open your ears and hear the plan that you may carry out what you have heard to accomplish what the Lord has put before you.

SELF-EVALUATION

1. Are you ready to win?
2. Did you hear the plans and strategy for victory from the Lord?
3. Did you get all of the plans?
4. Did you ask the questions that arose out of receiving the plan?

PRAYER

Dear Heavenly Father, the God of War who has never lost a battle. Who is the undefeated heavyweight of this world and universe! Lord, we ask You to give us a strategy for our victory. Lord, we ask You to uphold us in Your righteous right hand as you stretch out the left hand, causing the enemy to fall. The weapons we fight with are not the weapons of the world, but they have divine power to demolish strongholds (2 Corinthians 10:4). Lord send your lighting, causing a fire in the enemy camp that he may run and cause havoc within his camp. Let every dark force causing me suffering receive it back a thousandfold and, at the same time, release the Spirit of might and the fear of the Lord unto me. I ask all these things in Jesus's Holy name, Amen.

REFLECTION:

_____

_____

Heard

Ears to Proclaim God's Splendor

AFFIRMATION:

Revelations 21:7

He that overcometh shall inherit all things; and I will be his God, and he shall be my son.

PROCLAMATIONS:

Romans 8:37

Nay, in all these things we are more than conquerors through him that loved us.

Activations: Song Ten
Jesus Help Me!

Jesus help me to fulfill
What's been spoken unto me

Jesus help me to fulfill
What's been spoken unto me

Jesus help me to fulfill
What's been spoken unto me

Jesus help me to fulfill
What's been spoken unto me

SCRIPTURE SUPPORT

Fulfill
Matthew 26:54
How then will the Scriptures be fulfilled, which say that it must happen this way?

Psalm 22:1
To the chief Musician upon Aijeleth Shahar, A Psalm of David. My God, my God, why hast thou forsaken me? Why art thou so far from helping me, and from the words of my roaring?

Psalm 22:1 GOD'S WORD® Translation

[For the choir director; according to [ayyeleth hashachar]; a psalm by David.] My God, my God, why have you abandoned me? Why are you so far away from helping me, so far away from the words of my groaning?

Psalm 69:1
To the chief Musician upon Shoshannim, A Psalm of David. Save me, O God; for the waters are come in unto my soul

Psalm 69:1 GOD'S WORD® Translation
[For the choir director; according to [shoshannim]; by David.] Save me, O God! The water is already up to my neck!

Trust
Psalm 31:14
But I trusted in thee, O LORD: I said, Thou art my God...

Authority
Luke 10:19
Behold, I give unto you power to tread on serpents and scorpions, and overall the power of the enemy: and nothing shall by any means hurt you.

WORSHIP EXPRESSION

Have you ever had a time when you felt useless and weak? How about being separated from others. You're in a crowded room, but yet you feel alone. I was in that place when I began to hear this song. I was at my desk, and it was as if the choir of heaven was singing. Tears began to fill my eyes, and my body began to shake. I could feel the fire of the Lord running down my back. Lord Jesus is all I could say as I was pushed to the floor. I laid there crying and worshipping, singing this song. Whatever was trying to capture me was removed. The more I sang, the greater glory I felt. My mind became free, and I begin to transcend to a high place. The more I sang, the atmosphere changed; it was as if I was in the heavens. I walked by the waterfalls discussed in Revelations. The water was crystal blue, and behind the waterfall was a door. I thought to myself, what is behind the door? My mind began to question where I was. I recognized that I had been taken into a vision. I will discuss more in the closing of this book; every time I encounter Heaven, there is music. As I discuss at the beginning of the book, the sound of worship is the primary source of communication in Heaven. For were created to worship, and everything made by the Lord honors Him. After this experience, I began to feel greater glory when I prayed as well as more signs of my sonship with signs and wonders and miracles when I prayed for others. Allow His raw worship to take you unto greater glory.

SELF-EVALUATION

1. What did the song invoke in you?
2. Did you receive your help?
3. What did you hear after you studied this activation?

PRAYER

Dear Heavenly Father, the maker of all things, we thank You for the prophetic songs of deliverance so that the fulfillment of

Heard

our lives is accomplished. Lord, help us to surrender our will unto Your will that You can shift our mind and take us into a more significant place that Your works can rest upon us. Lord, open our ears that as we carry out Your appointment, we will hear Your steps clearer than ever. Lord, we desire to see You in new ways, but we must listen to You in new ways to effectively see you. Help us, Lord, to be the kingdom workers You have called us to be, in Jesus' Holy name, Amen.

REFLECTION:

_____
_____
_____
_____
_____
_____
_____
_____
_____
_____
_____
_____

Ears to Proclaim God's Splendor

AFFIRMATION:

Luke 4:18-19

The Spirit of the Lord is upon me, because he hath anointed me to preach the gospel to the poor; he hath sent me to heal the brokenhearted, to preach deliverance to the captives, and recovering of sight to the blind, to set at liberty them that are bruised, ¹⁹ To preach the acceptable year of the Lord.

EARS TO PROCLAIM GOD'S SPLENDOR

PROCLAMATIONS:

Isaiah 42:1

Behold my servant, whom I uphold; mine elect, in whom my soul delighteth; I have put my spirit upon him: he shall bring forth judgment to the Gentiles.

Isaiah 61:1-3

The Spirit of the Lord God is upon me; because the Lord hath anointed me to preach good tidings unto the meek; he hath sent me to bind up the brokenhearted, to proclaim liberty to the captives, and the opening of the prison to them that are bound;² To proclaim the acceptable year of the Lord, and the day of vengeance of our God; to comfort all that mourn; ³ To appoint unto them that mourn in Zion, to give unto them beauty for ashes, the oil of joy for mourning, the garment of praise for the spirit of heaviness; that they might be called trees of righteousness, the planting of the Lord, that he might be glorified.

_____

_____

_____

_____

_____

Heard

LESSON 3

Hearer

THE HEARER EXEMPLIFIES OBEDIENCE because to be a hearer, you must also be a doer according to the Word of the Lord. James 1:22-24 says, "But be ye doers of the word, and not hearers only, deceiving your own selves. For if any be a hearer of the word and not a doer, he is like unto a man beholding his natural face in a glass: For he beholdeth himself, and goeth his way, and straightway forgetteth what manner of man he was." A hearer is a person who hears or listens to something. The word is also capable of perceiving sound or ability to receive news or information; learn.[1] To carry out or learn from what you heard is a great way to learn the character of your Lord. The keyword in the definition is to learn. Most of us don't learn from our encounters with the Lord; instead, we make them a mystical phenomenon that makes us appear separate or higher than our brother and sister. When we teach from what we have learned in the encounters, we demystify the Lord that more people will desire those experiences.

Everything we hear from the Lord has a purpose and is supposed to help us subdue and dominate the earth. However, if we are the only ones subduing because we do not share what we learned, how can we truly dominate the world, remember we are one body with many members. With each member contributing a piece of the puzzle, the body can do more wondrous works than was done the day before. No more experiences when one person is out front doing all the demonstration as if they are the only one with power when the Word says Jesus died that we all would have access. Therefore, I compel you as your sister in Christ to not just read and get activated in hearing but take notes to learn that you can bring revelation unto another that we can truly work out the more remarkable works the Lord has before us.

These are the things I've learned to do during and after encounters with the Lord. Take note of everything seen, felt, smelled, and even heard. Then begin to compare with the biblical account: what is in the Bible, or did the Lord reveal a more in-depth revelation? That still can be compared with the Bible but may take more study. Remember, the Lord's Word is living, and things that live expand because they are forever adapting to the world's conditions. Now that you have the revelation, add it into your teaching and discuss it with those close to you. Remember, you know in part; thus, your brother or sister has a piece that you may not have a grasp. As the Word says, there is wisdom in counsel (Job 12:13). Therefore, let counsel be yours, and sound knowledge is your understanding. Let your ears be open to being a hearer like never before.

EARS TO PROCLAIM GOD'S SPLENDOR

SCRIPTURES TO MEDITATE ON HEARER

1. Romans 2:13
   a. (For not the hearers of the law are just before God, but the doers of the law shall be justified.
2. Ephesians 4:29
   a. Let no corrupt communication proceed out of your mouth, but that which is useful to the use of edifying, that it may minister grace unto the hearers.
3. James 1:23
   a. For if any be a hearer of the word and not a doer, he is like unto a man beholding his natural face in a glass:
4. James 1:25
   a. But whoso looketh into the perfect law of liberty, and continueth therein, he being not a forgetful hearer, but a doer of the work, this man shall be blessed in his deed.

Activations :Song Eleven
Let it be Me

Let it be Me
Let it be Me
Oh Lord, Let it be Me

Choose Me
Choose Me
Oh Lord, Please Choose Me

To do your will

To impart your skills
OH Lord - Let it be Me

Let it be Me
Let it be Me
Oh Lord, Let it be Me

Choose Me
Choose Me
Oh Lord, Please Choose Me
To do your will
To impart your skills
OH Lord, Let it be Me

SCRIPTURE SUPPORT

Chosen
Matthew 22:14
For many are called, but few are chosen.

Equip
Ephesians 4:10-12 (BSB)
He who descended is the very One who ascended above all the heavens in order to fill all things. ¹¹And it was He who gave some to be apostles, some to be prophets, some to be evangelists, and some to be pastors and teachers, ¹²to equip the saints for works of ministry and to build up the body of Christ

WORSHIP EXPRESSION

This song brought great delight. What a delight it is to be chosen? Chosen with a purpose that will help all you serve. First saved from the enemy's destruction and then placed on your feet and trained on following the Lord—then being sent the Holy Spirit. To not just dwell on the outside but inside to lead you to all truth. The truth of God that unlocks your internal call with gifts and titles from on high. All my life, I thought no one loved me to find my greatest over was my Savior. It can all be overwhelming at times, but I've learned to let the Lord be in control and to do my part, for Jesus has already completed the work. It is my job to follow what he has set in place. Are you asking the Lord to let it be you that brings healing to those connected to you or those you passed along the way? Remember, those who do the will of the Lord will obtain favor from Him. Not just acceptance for acting as if you're doing a great job but by doing the first things. First, seek the Lord and all His righteousness and then tell the world of His marvelous splendor.

SELF-EVALUATION

1. What did the song invoke in you?
2. Do you remember when the Lord called you?
3. Are you ready for what is next?

PRAYER

Dear Heavenly Father, the creator of all things, thank You for first choosing us even when we had no clue of what You were unto us. Thank You for teaching us reverence unto you. Lord, activate ears not just to hear but to listen. Compel us to take notes that help us to completely understand You. Lord, whatever thy will is to be doing, please do it with us. Teach us how to fulfill our lifes' calling, revealing all truth about us unto us. Please help us become equipped to equip another that the cycle of discipleship will never end, and the Kingdom would expand over the works of darkness, in Jesus' Holy Name, Amen.

REFLECTION:

Ears to Proclaim God's Splendor

AFFIRMATION:

John 17:21 (BSB)

That all of them may be one, as You, Father, are in Me, and I am in You. May they also be in Us, so that the world may believe that You sent Me.

Ears to Proclaim God's Splendor

PROCLAMATIONS:

John 17:15-26

I pray not that thou shouldest take them out of the world, but that thou shouldest keep them from the evil.

16 They are not of the world, even as I am not of the world.

17 Sanctify them through thy truth: thy word is truth.

18 As thou hast sent me into the world, even so have I also sent them into the world.

19 And for their sakes I sanctify myself, that they also might be sanctified through the truth.

20 Neither pray I for these alone, but for them also which shall believe on me through their word;

21 That they all may be one; as thou, Father, art in me, and I in thee, that they also may be one in us: that the world may believe that thou hast sent me.

22 And the glory which thou gavest me I have given them; that they may be one, even as we are one:

23 I in them, and thou in me, that they may be made perfect in one; and that the world may know that thou hast sent me, and hast loved them, as thou hast loved me.

24 Father, I will that they also, whom thou hast given me, be with me where I am; that they may behold my glory, which thou hast given me: for thou lovedst me before the foundation of the world.

25 O righteous Father, the world hath not known thee: but I have known thee, and these have known that thou hast sent me.

26 And I have declared unto them thy name and will declare it: that the love wherewith thou hast loved me may be in them, and I in them.

Ears to Proclaim God's Splendor

Activation: Song Twelve
I'm Blessed

I'm Blessed
I'm Blessed
No matter where the winds may blow
No matter if it's high or low
I'm Blessed
I'm Blessed

Here we go
Here we go
I'm Blessed
Here we go

No matter where the winds may blow
No matter if it high or low
No matter if it's east or west
My God is still the best

I'm blessed
Mmm -mmm – mmm
Oh – oh – oh
I'm blessed
No matter where he goes
My God still blesses the best
I'm blessed
Mmm -mmm – mmm
Oh – oh – oh

I'm blessed

SCRIPTURE SUPPORT

Needs Supplied
Philippians 4:19-20

But my God shall supply all your needs according to his riches in glory by Christ Jesus. Now unto God and our Father be glory for ever and ever. Amen.

Perfect Gift
James 1:17-18 (NIV)

Every good and perfect gift is from above, coming down from the Father of the heavenly lights, who does not change like shifting shadows. He chose to give us birth through the word of truth, that we might be a kind of firstfruits of all he created.

WORSHIP EXPRESSION

The more time I spend with the Lord, the more I understand His gifts are perfect. That doesn't mean I understand everything He gives me. However, if I desire to understand, He will show me the purpose because His desire is for all to fulfill the plans He placed in us before we were ever in our mother's womb. This song came as I began to understand my calling and took the limits off what the Lord had for me. I used to say, "Okay, this is all I'm called unto," until this song deposited into me. I could hear the Lord saying to me, "Child, nothing in you is simple, and everything I called unto you is excellent. Great because I called it and destined it before you were ever conceived, thus proving the vastness of my glory." This song comes to me everytime I try to minimize something God is doing in my life. Allow yourself to hear what astonishing and perfect thing the Lord is perfecting in you that you will understand the magnitude of the call on your life.

SELF-EVALUATION

1. Do you believe you are blessed?
2. Did you believe you have a great purpose?
3. What did you hear after you studied this activation?

PRAYER

Dear Heavenly Father, the lover of our soul—the God who didn't just create us of purpose but for purpose. A drive within us that will birth great things within this world. Lord activate the plan within me. Allow them to come forth that I will understand Your will for my life. Help me to grasp nothing you have called me to do is small. Help me not to be jealous of other's calls, for that is the character of the devil. But Lord, clean out the world's behaviors and pour into me your fruit that I may bear seed that will allow you to bring a significant increase to all that I encounter, in your Son Jesus' Holy name, amen.

REFLECTION:

_____

_____

Ears to Proclaim God's Splendor

Hearer

AFFIRMATION:

Deuteronomy 28:1-7

And it shall come to pass, if thou shalt hearken diligently unto the voice of the Lord thy God, to observe and to do all his commandments which I command thee this day, that the Lord thy God will set thee on high above all nations of the earth:

2 And all these blessings shall come on thee, and overtake thee if thou shalt hearken unto the voice of the Lord thy God.

3 Blessed shalt thou be in the city and blessed shalt thou be in the field.

4 Blessed shall be the fruit of thy body, and the fruit of thy ground, and the fruit of thy cattle, the increase of thy kine, and the flocks of thy sheep.

5 Blessed shall be thy basket and thy store.

6 Blessed shalt thou be when thou comest in, and blessed shalt thou be when thou goest out.

7 The Lord shall cause thine enemies that rise up against thee to be smitten before thy face: they shall come out against thee one way, and flee before thee seven ways.

Hearer

PROCLAMATIONS:

Deuteronomy 28:8-14

The Lord shall command the blessing upon thee in thy storehouses, and in all that thou settest thine hand unto; and he shall bless thee in the land which the Lord thy God giveth thee.

9 The Lord shall establish thee an holy people unto himself, as he hath sworn unto thee, if thou shalt keep the commandments of the Lord thy God, and walk in his ways.

10 And all people of the earth shall see that thou art called by the name of the Lord; and they shall be afraid of thee.

11 And the Lord shall make thee plenteous in goods, in the fruit of thy body, and in the fruit of thy cattle, and in the fruit of thy ground, in the land which the Lord sware unto thy fathers to give thee.

12 The Lord shall open unto thee his good treasure, the heaven to give the rain unto thy land in his season, and to bless all the work of thine hand: and thou shalt lend unto many nations, and thou shalt not borrow.

13 And the Lord shall make thee the head, and not the tail; and thou shalt be above only, and thou shalt not be beneath; if that thou hearken unto the commandments of the Lord thy God, which I command thee this day, to observe and to do them:

14 And thou shalt not go aside from any of the words which I command thee this day, to the right hand, or to the left, to go after other gods to serve them.

Activation: Song Thirteen
Oh, How I Worship you

Oh How I worship in your Glory
You are my mighty king
Oh, How I worship you
Oh How I worship in your Glory
You are my mighty - mighty king
In your presence, you bring everything
In your presence is where I see
You for what you are to me
Oh, How I worship you
Oh, How I love to be in your presence
Oh, How I love to be in your presence my King
OH, How I worship in your Glory
You are a mighty God
You are a mighty God
Oh, How I simply worship you

SCRIPTURE SUPPORT

Worship
Hebrews 13:15

By him, therefore, let us offer the sacrifice of praise to God continually, that is, the fruit of our lips giving thanks to his name.

Sacrifice
Psalm 50:14

Sacrifice a thank offering to God, and fulfill your vows to the Most High.

WORSHIP EXPRESSION

The easiest way to get clarity from the Lord is to worship. Let me proclaim that worshiping in spirit and truth is the most incredible way to clear out unclean spirits. For the Lord loves to inhabit His people's praises; thus, nothing unholy can dwell in that praise. Since the Lord doesn't come without purpose, He will leave more than you ever imagine during His visit. He will usher out the old and bring in the new that you will be prepared to worship Him within more significant measure for all to see. The overflow of your worship will touch all that comes within that place because where the Lord's presence is, there is power for you and all who desire to be changed.

SELF-EVALUATION

1. What did the song raise in you?
2. Is the spirit of worship there?
3. What did you hear after you studied this activation?

PRAYER

Dear Heavenly Father, the Lord over the heavens and earth, we worship You with every facet of our being. Lord, we adore You with all we have. Lord, place us upon our feet and show us all concerning what you have for us. Lord, we don't ask for anything but You. That You will dwell with us a more significant

Ears to Proclaim God's Splendor

magnitude that You change us to have hearts and minds like Yours, Lord. Fulfill the promise of victory, Lord, not just for ourselves but for Your glory, in Jesus Holy name, Amen.

REFLECTION:

_____

_____

_____

_____

_____

_____

_____

_____

_____

_____

_____

_____

_____

_____

_____

Hearer

EARS TO PROCLAIM GOD'S SPLENDOR

AFFIRMATION:

Hebrews 12:28 (BSB)

Therefore, since we are receiving an unshakable kingdom, let us be filled with gratitude, and so worship God acceptably with reverence and awe.

PROCLAMATIONS:

1 Peter 2:5

You also, like living stones, are being built into a spiritual house to be a holy priesthood, offering spiritual sacrifices acceptable to God through Jesus Christ.

Activation: Song Fourteen
I Shall Decree

I shall decree
My Promise
of what the Lord will do
I shall decree my victory
For Armies of the Lord will bring me through
I shall hear my Lord cry out for me
Daughter, you are free

I shall decree my victory before this world and unto you
I shall decree my promises of what the Lord will do
I shall say them all
no matter what you do
My Lord - My Lord will bring me through

I shall decree my victory before the Lord bring me through
I shall decree my promises for what he is going to do
For he has a plan for me, and you
I shall decree
I shall decree what the Lord will do

SCRIPTURE SUPPORT

Decree
Job 22:28

Thou shalt also decree a thing, and it shall be established unto thee: and the light shall shine upon thy ways.

Light Shined
Psalm 97:11
Light is sown on the righteous, gladness on the upright in heart.

WORSHIP EXPRESSION

After I had been praying for the list given by the Lord, this song was dropped on me to show me what He wanted me to establish on the earth. I can be honest; I was complaining that He was asking me to do things blindly. I am nosey. I love asking the Lord questions, and it's rare for Him not to show me, but after the process, I understood. He was teaching me yet another lesson. However, it wasn't long before this song came reminding me of my job, and that was to decree a thing, and it would be established. Yes, I'm guilty of trying to do the Lord's job, but He has no problem checking me because I'm His child and putting me back in right standing so that I may continue upon the path He has created for me. Sometimes our lack of understanding mixed with our flesh can get in the way. Just know that you will do great things, but there is a formula to receive. Therefore confess out of your mouth what you desire to see and allow the Lord to drop newfound understanding as you sit ready to listen to declare to all who has an ear to hear.

SELF-EVALUATION

1. Are you complaining or worshipping unto the Father?
2. Once you confessed where you indeed are in Christ, what did you hear?

3. Receive your song of declaration in Jesus' name, Amen.

PRAYER

Dear Heavenly Father, the Lord that established heaven and earth, we thank You for the opportunity to cleanse ourselves before You. Lord, we lay down every curse spoken out of our mouths. Lord, help us not get caught up in what we are going through but to stay focused on the help coming to fulfill every promise. Lord, allow us to hear your soothing sounds of declaration that will give personal birth deliverance, healing, and breakthrough. We ask all these things in Jesus' Holy Name, amen.

REFLECTION:

_____

_____

_____

_____

_____

_____

_____

_____

Hearer

EARS TO PROCLAIM GOD'S SPLENDOR

AFFIRMATION:

Job 11:17 (BSB)
Your life will be brighter than the noonday; its darkness will be like the morning.

PROCLAMATIONS:

Job 33:28 (BSB)
He redeemed my soul from going down to the Pit, and I will live to see the light.'

Activation: Song fifteen
Blessed It Be the Child

Blessed it be the child
The mighty child
Oh, the mighty child
Blessed it be the child

Blessed it be the King
The mighty King
Oh, the mighty King
Blessed it be the King

Blessed it be the Lamb
The mighty Lamb
Oh, the mighty Lamb
Blessed it be the Lamb

Blessed it be the Name
The mighty Name
Oh, the mighty Name
Blessed it be the name of Jesus
The Name above everything

SCRIPTURE SUPPORT

Giving Thanks
1 Thessalonians 5:16-18

Rejoice evermore. 17 Pray without ceasing. 18 In everything give thanks: for this is the will of God in Christ Jesus concerning you.

Rejoice
Philippians 4:4
Rejoice in the Lord always. I will say it again: Rejoice!

WORSHIP EXPRESSION

Thinking about this song brings tears to my eyes. I received this song during a heavenly encounter. As you read, every interaction with the Lord is an opportunity to learn and clarify your identity. This encounter is the very foundation of that statement within this vision/dream. I call it this because I was like Paul when he says he was in or out of the body he doesn't know (2 Corinthians 12). That is how it was with this encounter. I was praying, and then I began to wait for the Lord to answer, and then I was seated at the end of a bed in a cave. The cave was symbolic of the Lord hiding me because He had me in training. Thus, many had no clue who I truly am, and still today, I have very few who God gives access to see me. Some of you reading this would say that an arrogant statement; however, it is actually in great humility because that is how the Lord keeps me hidden. If anyone can see who you are, how can you stay hidden from the devil? Remember not everyone that cries Lord - Lord is walking after the heart of the Lord.

During this third heaven encounter, was instructed how to carry out my ministry and walk. I know most are saying what the instructions were. You will soon read about it, keep reading my books. After getting the teaching, and I noticed that Jesus was present, I began to hear this song, and my body melted once I acknowledged what I was hearing. It was as if I was dead. Not my spirit but my body because my body could not withstand that Holy place. Another reason why we will get glorified bodies. Two angels usher me closer to the throne. It is a beautiful place.

Once I awakened or came to, my physical body was shaking. That is why I don't know if I was in or out of the body. I felt as if I had been there, really not just dreaming; however, since I cannot be sure, I will state what my brother Paul said as listed above. However, the song I heard stuck, and still, today, if I begin to feel the absence of the Lord, I sing this song and the glory fire rushes back upon me.

SELF-EVALUATION

1. Could you hear the song as you read my expression?
2. Did you hear the angels singing over this song?
3. What did you hear after you studied this activation?

PRAYER

Dear Heavenly Father, the maker of all things, we thank You for the prophetic song of entry into greater glory and power. Lord, help us to surrender our will unto Your will that You can shift our minds and take us into a more excellent place that Your works can rest upon us. Lord, open our ears that as we carry out Your assignments, we will hear Your steps clearer than ever before. Lord, we desire to see You in new ways, but we must listen to You in new ways to effectively see You. Help us, Lord, to be the Kingdom workers You have called us to be, in Jesus' Holy name, Amen.

REFLECTION:

_____
_____
_____
_____
_____
_____
_____
_____
_____
_____
_____
_____
_____
_____

Ears to Proclaim God's Splendor

AFFIRMATION:

Romans 12:12
Rejoicing in hope; patient in tribulation; continuing instant in prayer;

Ears to Proclaim God's Splendor

PROCLAMATIONS:

Ephesians 6:18 (BSB)

Pray in the Spirit at all times, with every kind of prayer and petition. To this end, stay alert with all perseverance in your prayers for all the saints.

LESSON 4

Hearest

FOR ALL THOSE WHO are English majors, yes, you see the word correctly "hearest". This word is an action word for those who walk in the Spirit desiring the mysteries of the Kingdom of heaven and not those who seek intelligence based on this world system or religious traditions. Can thou ear hearest the secrets? Do you hear those who have charge over us carrying out the will of the Lord. If your answer is no, then my question is do you desire to hear? This book is not just about hearing what one can comprehend but hearing what one cannot, which requires you to rely on the Lord. Thinking about the time when you needed prayer but knew not what though required, it was your mourns and groans that interceded for you.

Romans 8:26 (BSB) states, "In the same way, the Spirit helps us in our weakness. For we do not know how we ought to pray, but the Spirit Himself intercedes for us with groans too deep for words." Think about this, your body hears what is needed and intercedes. Thus, the body does have its own will. That is why the Lord tells us not to give unto the appetite of the flesh because if you have been feeding your body the world, it will long for it; however, if you cleanse your body with the Word of God, it desires after the things of God. Therefore, I announce Psalm 145:21. "My mouth will declare the praise of the LORD; let every creature bless His holy name forever and ever. That I always with everything I am hearest the Lord that I may carry out what He has for me within that moment." Within that moment could be the second that brings deliverance for another. To hear the answer to a problem or even get the life-changing healing. The honor to hear the Lord's desires for another. To listen to the breakthrough that can take a person from darkness to light. Hearing not for yourself but demonstrate Christ for all those who yearn to know Him, showing them what you have heard because of your relationship and willingness to listen and obey what you have heard that another may hearest the call of the Lord. May you be activated to hear in prayer, worship, and even while the preaching is going forth. Let your ears be open to hearing Him within all things.

SCRIPTURES TO MEDITATE ON "HEAREST"

1. Psalm 65:2
    a. O thou that hearest prayer, unto thee shall all flesh come.

2. John 3:8
    a. The wind bloweth where it listeth, and thou hearest the sound thereof, but canst not tell whence it cometh, and whither it goeth: so is every one that is born of the Spirit.

3. John 11:42
    a. And I knew that thou hearest me always: but because of the people which stand by I said it, that they may believe that thou hast sent me.

<u>Activations: Song Sixteen</u>
We worship You

We worship You
Oh, Mighty God
King of Kings
Lord of Lords

We worship You
Oh, Mighty God
King of Kings
Lord of Lords

King of Kings
Lord of Lords
You are worthy of our praise
Worthy of our praise

We worship you
Oh, Mighty God
King of Kings
Lord of Lords

SCRIPTURE SUPPORT

Worship
Isaiah 25:1

O Lord, thou art my God; I will exalt thee, I will praise thy name; for thou hast done wonderful things; thy counsels of old are faithfulness and truth.

King of Kings
1 Timothy 6:15

Which in his times he shall shew, who is the blessed and only Potentate, the King of kings, and Lord of lords.

WORSHIP EXPRESSION

This song was released unto me while I was teaching. Often after I've been led by the Holy Spirit, the Lord gives me a song. These songs are a mark from God; they're a way of saying a job well done and on to the next topic. I can say that because I've been teaching, and all of a sudden, I can hear a song. and I'm like, "Lord, I'm not done," but the music will get louder and louder, letting me know to move on to what He is showing me prophetically. The song doesn't always come at the end, sometimes in the beginning or even in the middle, but as soon as I hear them, I know the Lord is present and will move powerfully. The more you learn to listen, the more you will learn how the Lord uses you to demonstrate His power. Mine just so happen to be music; He uses music to communicate what He wants. I've learned how to follow the music because I've learned how to trust Him. I've also learned cause it never fails; God heals and delivers at a greater rate when the music shows up.

SELF-EVALUATION

1. What is your primary form of communication with the Lord?
2. If you don't know, ask the Lord to show you?
3. Listen closely, and you will be surprised by the methods He uses.
4. What did you hear after you studied this activation?

PRAYER

Dear Heavenly Father, the creator of every sound upon the earth, we thank You for the wind, rain, snow, and even thunder. All have their unique display of Your glory. Lord, help us see the unique communication form that allows us to know You in ways we never imagine. Lord, activate us to listen to hear You in every way you choose to communicate. Open our minds and hearts to receive You. We pray against the fear of new things and fear of the unknown, and we rest in Your arms of activation of every part of us to know You on new levels, in Jesus' Holy Name, amen.

REFLECTION:

_____

_____

_____

Ears to Proclaim God's Splendor

Hearest

Ears to Proclaim God's Splendor

AFFIRMATION:

Deuteronomy 10:17

For the LORD, your God is God of gods and Lord of lords, the great, mighty, and awesome God, showing no partiality and accepting no bribe.

PROCLAMATIONS:

Proverbs 8:15
By me, kings reign, and princes decree justice.

Activation: Song Seventeen
Blessed it Be the Lord

Blessed it be the Lord
Blessed it be the Lord
Blessed it be the Lord
Blessed it be the Lord
Blessed it be the Lord
Blessed it be the Lord

King of Kings
Lord of Lords
King of Kings
Lord of Lords
King of Kings
Lord of Lords

Blessed it be the Lord
Blessed it be the Lord
Blessed it be the Lord
Blessed it be the Lord
Blessed it be the Lord
Blessed it be the Lord

SCRIPTURE SUPPORT

Serve God
Psalm 72:11

Yea, all kings shall fall down before him: all nations shall serve him.

Glorify
Psalm 86:9 (BSB)
All the nations You have made will come and bow before You, O Lord, and they will glorify Your name.

WORSHIP EXPRESSION

My favorite time with the Lord is our one-on-one time. When the Lord and I fellowship together, I can be myself and tell Him everything in my heart. For Him to respond is beyond anything I have ever come upon. It was the Holy Ghost that began to talk to me one day while in a sad place. I was crying yet again about the suffering of life, and just when I thought there was no hope, I heard the Holy Ghost say, "You don't have to cry anymore." It was actually in words the first time and then sung the second time. When I asked Him to repeat what I heard, I was in shock, but I felt comfort as I repeated what I heard, and my tears stopped. It wasn't long after that I was delivered out of that place of no hope. The Lord vindicated me just as He does all the time. My deliverance was first received directly from the Holy Ghost.

SELF-EVALUATION

1. Where do you lack hope?
2. Have you asked the Holy Spirit to help you in that area?

3. Are you ready to be activated to hear not just for others but yourself?
4. What did you hear after you studied this activation?

PRAYER

Dear Heavenly Father of all things, we thank You for the prophetic song of entry into hope and deliverance. We thank You that even when people have no words, You can come and deliver Your Spirit that can bring miracles into our lives and the life of others. We thank You for never leaving us in broken places and having an ear to hear us first. You are a loving God that loves us more than we ever deserve. Lord, activate my ears to hear more than just for others but for myself that I may be a witness of not only what we speak but what we do, in Jesus' Holy name, Amen.

REFLECTION:

_____

_____

_____

_____

_____

_____

_____

Hearest

Ears to Proclaim God's Splendor

AFFIRMATION:

Psalm 138:4 (BSB)

All the kings of the earth will give You thanks, O LORD, when they hear the words of Your mouth.

PROCLAMATIONS:

Daniel 7:27 (BSB)
Then the sovereignty, dominion, and greatness of the kingdoms under all of heaven will be given to the people, the saints of the Most High. His kingdom will be an everlasting kingdom, and all rulers will serve and obey Him.'

Activation: Song Eighteen
Teach Us

Teach us how to love You
How to love you
Teach Us – Teach Us
Teach us how

Teach us how to trust You
How to trust You
Teach Us – Teach Us – Teach Us
Teach us how

Teach us how to obey You
How to obey You
Teach Us – Teach Us
Teach us how

Teach us How to follow You
How to follow You
Teach Us – Teach Us
Teach us how

SCRIPTURE SUPPORT

Teach
Colossians 3:16

Let the word of Christ dwell in you richly in all wisdom; teaching and admonishing one another in psalms and hymns and spiritual songs, singing with grace in your hearts to the Lord.

Train
Romans 10:17
Consequently, faith comes by hearing, and hearing by the word of Christ

Wisdom
Colossians 1:28 (BSB)
We proclaim Him, admonishing and teaching everyone with all wisdom, so that we may present everyone perfect in Christ.

WORSHIP EXPRESSION

I call this my very own teaching song. God gave me this song while praying for people. I asked the Lord to teach them how to carry out His truth and not get caught up in the world's facade and popular displays of prophetic teaching. As I finished praying, I could hear this song. The more I sang, the more the Holy Spirit added different things I wanted to see in those closest to me. In shock because I hadn't voiced the things. I simply followed the Holy Spirit and sang with my entire heart. The song brought so much encouragement. Sometimes as a teacher, it is hard to know if people are getting the information. We have people not looking to learn but looking for someone to accept their wrong way because the religious sector has pushed that if someone tells you that you are doing something wrong its judgment or if what they say doesn't please our itching ears that we don't have to accept the correction. However, regardless if we accept it or not, the Lord will hold us accountable for every teaching we decided not to learn. Accountability is a major thing missing in the body of Christ. Hearing from the Lord brings back that accountability because whether you like what was said or not, hearing from the Lord brings back individual spiritual responsibility. People can no longer hide behind; well, that word came from a man I can choose to listen to or not, and I will be okay because God knows my heart. The individual directly impacted with their heart checked when the Lord brings correction or reproof—helping believers become more confident in themselves and learning from leadership. The encounter also gives them less demonic attacks because the devil can not steal what the Lord has directly done. He can try, but the creation has met his Creator, and even if the individual wants to deny, the flesh will not.

SELF-EVALUATION

1. Are you teachable?
2. Do you hear natural and spiritual correction?
3. What did you hear after you studied this activation?

PRAYER

Dear Heavenly Father, the producer of all things, we thank You for not leaving us as unlearned beings and for your willingness to teach us even when we are not receptive to the teaching. Lord helps us hear not just what our itching ears want to hear but also listen to what is needed to shift us and those around us.

Please help us to be more Christ-like and less like the religious sectors around us. Help us to walk according to the Kingdom of God and not according to this world, in Jesus' Holy name, Amen.

REFLECTION:

… Ears to Proclaim God's Splendor

AFFIRMATION:

Ephesians 5:19 (BSB)
Speak to one another with psalms, hymns, and spiritual songs. Sing and make music in your hearts to the Lord,

PROCLAMATIONS:

1 Corinthians 14:15 (BSB)

What then shall I do? I will pray with my spirit, but I will also pray with my mind. I will sing with my spirit, but I will also sing with my mind.

Activation: Song Nineteen
The Anchor of my Soul

Bright Morning Star
The Holy One
The Anchor of my soul
Please come and take control

The Morning Star
That is who - You are
The Anchor of my soul
You can have full control

For there is nothing for me without you
That is why I give my life unto you

Bright Morning Star
The Holy One
The Anchor of My soul
Please come and take control

SCRIPTURE SUPPORT

Anchor
Hebrews 6:19
Which hope we have as an anchor of the soul, both sure and steadfast, and which entereth into that within the veil;

Proclaim

Ears to Proclaim God's Splendor

Romans 1:8 (BSB)

First, I thank my God through Jesus Christ for all of you, because your faith is being proclaimed all over the world.

Faith

1 Thessalonians 1:8 (BSB)

For not only did the message of the Lord ring out from you to Macedonia and Achaia, but your faith in God has gone out to every place, so that we have no need to say anything more.

WORSHIP EXPRESSION

This song came as a reminder my soul is anchored within the Lord. Being a person who was attacked by the spirit of rejection since birth, the enemy always strikes me with rejection from people. My most significant rejection comes from those I'm called to help. Many times the Lord has already shown me that they have no clue I'm here to help, so I must keep quiet and take the rejection until the Lord releases me to let them know why I'm truly there. Most of the time, I tell people when I first connect, but because most people don't listen when you talk to them. They don't hear what you say. I used to be this way, so I'm talking about myself, but the Holy Spirit didn't have it. I would get yelled at and asked to repeat what I heard. If I didn't repeat it correctly, then I would be in what I call "no talk." I wouldn't hear from the Holy Spirit until I gave the correct answer. Look, you learn quickly not to mess with the Holy Spirit. He is real and doesn't play. However, this lesson took my mind off the suffering of life because I had the Holy Spirit, a friend who knew the real me; thus, the world's rejection was not critical because my mind was on things above and not beneath.

SELF-EVALUATION

1. Do you proclaim the Lord in song?
2. Did you believe He has something new He wants to deposit in you?
3. What did you hear after you studied this activation?

PRAYER

Dear Heavenly Father of Heaven and Earth. We thank You for knowing just what we need to overcome the cares of this life. Lord help us listen and pray for one another at greater depth and not always look at our personal mindset. Man teaches superiority; however, Lord, You teach servanthood, for Your Son was the greatest man who lived; yet He never presented Himself as superior, but instead presented Himself as a servant. Please help us to have a servant mentality. Please help us to hear clearly from You in every area of our life. Help us know the purpose of those connected to us and not look at ourselves more highly than we ought to think, in Jesus' Holy name, Amen.

REFLECTION:

_____

_____

_____

Ears to Proclaim God's Splendor

AFFIRMATION:

1 Corinthians 1:4 (BSB)
I always thank my God for you because of the grace He has given you in Christ Jesus.

EARS TO PROCLAIM GOD'S SPLENDOR

PROCLAMATIONS:

Psalm 39:7
Now, Lord, for what do I wait? My hope is in You.

Activation: Song Twenty
Love

With Love and Kindness
I draw men to me
With Love and Kindness
I will set you free
It's Love
Love
Simply My Love

With Love and Kindness
I draw men to me
With Love and Kindness
I will set you free
It's Love
Love
Simply My Love

With Love and Kindness
I draw men to me
With Love and Kindness
I will set you free
It's Love
Love
Simply My Love

SCRIPTURE SUPPORT

Love of God

John 3:16

For God so loved the world, that he gave his only begotten Son, that whosoever believeth in him should not perish, but have everlasting life.

Kindness

Jeremiah 31:3

The LORD hath appeared of old unto me, saying, Yea, I have loved thee with an everlasting love: therefore, with lovingkindness have I drawn thee.

WORSHIP EXPRESSION

My favorite pastime is allowing the Glory of the Lord to fall on me. There are many times when it falls, and I'm not ready. You heard me correctly. I'm teaching or reading, and I feel the presence of the Lord come on my back. His favorite way to get my attention is for me to feel the fire on my back. The hotter the fire, the more urgent it is to get in my secret place. I learned to go when He calls so that I won't miss valuable information. Remember this is your God; you're not in control. He is- thus when He calls, get up and go. When the Glory falls, it's like I'm in another place, and everything from my hearing, sight and even my touch becomes more sensitive. This helps me know that I may teach others how to find them based on what God said and not what the world says. Can you hear as you read this the Lord inviting you into His secret place? I do; I listen to Him beckoning us to come that He can show us new and beautiful things beyond this world. Go and let the Spirit of the Lord fall on you.

SELF-EVALUATION

1. What did the song invoke in you?
2. Did you feel a greater glory?
3. What did you hear after you studied this activation?

PRAYER

Dear Heavenly Father, we love You more than the air we breathe. We love You because You first drew us with Your love and kindness when we were not so clean. Thank You, Lord, for always wanting to commune with us even when we sometimes ignore your call. Lord, help us to see, hear, and feel You in ways we never thought possible, in Jesus' Holy name, Amen.

REFLECTION:

_____
_____
_____
_____
_____
_____
_____

Ears to Proclaim God's Splendor

AFFIRMATION:

Hosea 11:4 (BSB)
I led them with cords of kindness, with ropes of love; I lifted the yoke from their necks and bent down to feed them.

EARS TO PROCLAIM GOD'S SPLENDOR

PROCLAMATIONS:

Malachi 1:2 (BSB)

"I have loved you," says the LORD. But you ask, "How have You loved us?" "Was not Esau Jacob's brother?" declares the LORD. "Yet Jacob I have loved,

LESSON 5

Heareth

THE WORD HEARETH PERTAINS to the Lord calling you, and you are not in worship or prayer. Do you know the Lord wants to talk to you throughout the day and night? To hear the Lord call you by name is beyond anything you have ever heard before. Like young Samuel, most of us will look for a person because we are unfamiliar with God's voice and presence. It is like when you hear your parents call you. You can tell how they use your name if you're in trouble well as you get used to the Lord's calling. You will get to know Him well enough that you can simply say yes, Lord, and await His reply. This lesson is to activate you to hear the Lord's call, no matter the time of day or hour. You will be a sheep that can heareth, and you will respond to your Lord. You may hear Him call you in a dream or vision no matter you will know His voice. You may hear Him call you in the day or night but each time His call will awaken you. No matter the time, you will know His voice. You will see the voice of your God respond with what He needs from thee.

SCRIPTURES TO MEDITATE ON HEARETH

Ears to Proclaim God's Splendor

1. 1 Samuel 3:9-10
   a. Therefore Eli said unto Samuel, Go, lie down: and it shall be, if he call thee, that thou shalt say, Speak, Lord; for thy servant heareth. So Samuel went and lay down in his place. And the Lord came, and stood, and called as at other times, Samuel, Samuel. Then Samuel answered, Speak; for thy servant heareth.

2. Psalm 34:17
   a. The righteous cry and the Lord heareth, and delivereth them out of all their troubles.

3. Proverb 13:8
   a. The ransom of a man's life are his riches: but the poor heareth not rebuke.

4. Luke 10:16
   a. He that heareth you heareth me; and he that despiseth you despiseth me; and he that despiseth me despiseth him that sent me.

5. John 9:31
   a. Now we know that God heareth not sinners: but if any man be a worshipper of God, and doeth his will, him, he heareth.

6. John 18:37
   a. Pilate therefore said unto him, Art thou a king then? Jesus answered, Thou sayest that I am a king. To this end was I born, and for this cause came I into the

world, that I should bear witness unto the truth. Every one that is of the truth heareth my voice.

7. 1 John 4:6
    a. We are of God: he that knoweth God heareth us; he that is not of God heareth not us. Hereby know we the spirit of truth, and the spirit of error.

8. Revelations 22:17
    a. And the Spirit and the bride say, Come. And let him that heareth say, Come. And let him that is a thirst come. And whosoever will, let him take the water of life freely.

Activations Song Twenty-One
Fall On me

Fall on me
Fall on me

Fall afresh Lord
I need your Glory, Lord
I need your Power, Lord

Fall on me
Fall afresh on me
Fall afresh on me
Cleanse my mind, Lord
Fall on me
Cleanse my heart, Lord

Fall on me
Fall fresh on me
Purify me, Lord
Fall on me
For use Lord

Fall on Me
Fall afresh On me
On me
I need you Oh Lord
Fall on me
There is no one Greater Lord
Fall on me
Fall afresh on me
Fall afresh on me

SCRIPTURE SUPPORT

The Beloved
Ephesians 1:6
To the praise of the glory of his grace, wherein he hath made us accepted in the beloved.

Redemption
Ephesians 1:7
In whom we have redemption through his blood, the forgiveness of sins, according to the riches of his grace.

Spiritual Hope

Ephesians 1:12

That we should be to the praise of his glory, who first trusted in Christ.

WORSHIP EXPRESSION

I was feeling lonely and isolated, and then the song came unto me. Have you ever heard the expression in a crowd full of people, but you still feel alone? That was me during this time. The more I studied God's Word and worshipped, the more separated I thought from the Lord. I needed a touch from the Father. I needed Him to come and wrap His arms around me. Nothing else would do. I prayed, begging the Lord to go for days. I keep reading His Word, worshipping, and praying. I know my actions would draw the Father. I knew he would have to go because I would continue to knock, ask, and seek until He showed up to meet me. Then finally, in the middle of the night, I began to feel a presence upon me. As I laid on my stomach, I felt hands on my shoulders that awoke me. These hands were so gentle. I looked to my right, thinking it was my husband but knowing it was not because this touch was different. As the hand patted me on my back, I began to hear these words. Tears began to flow, and I felt every ounce of absence leave.

My heart began to burn, and from that moment, I began to feel the Lord deeper than ever before. The Lord often deals with me in the fire. He met me for the first time with fire and saved me, and He continues to meet me with fire, gradually bringing me to the place He has destined for me.

SELF-EVALUATION

1. Have you ever longed for the touch of the Father? How did you obtain His touch?
2. Are you desperate to see Him in new ways?
3. Do you believe there are things God can show you beyond your understanding?
4. Have you asked Him for the mysteries of His Kingdom?

PRAYER

Dear Heavenly Father, the Father of all things, the lover of our soul and the ruler of all things. For You are the Holy One (Mark 1:24), we come today laying at Your feet asking You yet again to be the rock of our salvation (1 Cor 10:4). Help us trust You and walk in the right motives that we will receive when we ask because we are not asking amiss. We are not coming to ask for things that will bring pleasure unto ourselves, but we ask to be of use unto the Father. Trusting the Lord with our whole hearts and leaning not unto our understanding but acknowledging Him in all our ways. The God of the way, the truth, and the life (James 14:6). Open our ears to hear not just of this world but unto your Heaven that we will not miss anything you have for us in Jesus' holy name, I pray. Amen.

REFLECTION:

_____

_____

Heareth

Ears to Proclaim God's Splendor

AFFIRMATION:

Psalm 130:7 (BSB)

O Israel, put your hope in the LORD, for with the LORD is loving devotion, and with Him is redemption in abundance.

PROCLAMATIONS:

Matthew 6:12
And forgive us our debts, as we also have forgiven our debtors.

Activation: Song Twenty-Two
You Got to Go

Pain You Got to Go
I said, pain, You got to go
I said pain; You got to go
The pain you go to go
In Jesus Name

We say pain, you got to go
We said, pain, you got to go
We said pain, and you got to go
Pain you got to go
In Jesus Name

SCRIPTURE SUPPORT

Grace
2 Corinthians 12:9

And he said unto me, My grace is sufficient for thee: for my strength is made perfect in weakness. Most gladly, therefore, will I rather glory in my infirmities, that the power of Christ may rest upon me.

God's Power
1 Corinthians 2:5 (BSB)

so that your faith would not rest on men's wisdom but God's power.

Strength
Philippians 4:13 (BSB)
I can do all things through Christ who gives me strength.

Healed
Isaiah 53:5
But he was wounded for our transgressions, he was bruised for our iniquities: the chastisement of our peace was upon him; and with his stripes we are healed.

WORSHIP EXPRESSION

In the middle of teaching, this song came bursting through like fire. I began to get a prophetic download about the pain and suffering of someone present while I was teaching. Her grief was great; however, the Lord directed me to declare all of the suffering and pain to flee. Not by my own might but by His Spirit speaking things as if they should be. Breaking off the demonic and cycle of torcher that the enemy loves to keep us in. The songs that we hear are not just for us but for others. The more you get used to hearing from on high, the more you will learn the purpose of the songs given. It is part of building your relationship with your King of Kings and Lord of Lords, allowing Him to teach you while you teach others actively.

SELF-EVALUATION

1. Do you have pain in your life?
2. Are there those around you suffering from pain?

3. Do you hear a song of healing and deliverance for the pain?

PRAYER

Dear Heavenly Father of Heaven and Earth. Thank You for being God and loving us. Thank You for coming and suffering for our name's sake. Thank You for every lash by which I am made free. Lord, we come against every form of pain in our lives, and we ask Your blood to go and cover us healing us, for You have already paid the price. Lord, let us hear what You have to say about the pain around us that we may have a counter when the enemy tries to bring pain into our lives or bring back past hurts. I pray all of these things in Jesus' holy name. Amen.

REFLECTION:

_____

_____

_____

_____

_____

_____

_____

_____

Heareth

Ears to Proclaim God's Splendor

AFFIRMATION:

2 Corinthians 3:5

Not that we are sufficient of ourselves to think anything as of ourselves; but our sufficiency is of God;

PROCLAMATIONS:

1 Peter 2:24 (BSB)

He Himself bore our sins in His body on the tree, so that we might die to sin and live to righteousness. "By His stripes you are healed."

Activation: Song Twenty-Three
Take Your Place

Lord come and take your place
Come and fill this place
We need your warm embrace
Come Lord – Take your place

Lord come and take your place
Come and fill this place
We need your warm embrace
Come Lord – Take your place

Lord come and take your place
Come and fill this place
We need your warm embrace
Come Lord – Take your place

SCRIPTURE SUPPORT

Alpha & Omega
Revelation 22:13

I am Alpha and Omega, the beginning and the end, the first and the last.

Holy Spirit fill this Place
Ezekiel 43:5

So, the spirit took me up, and brought me into the inner court; and, behold, the glory of the Lord filled the house.

Glory Appearance
Ezekiel 1:28 (BSB)

The appearance of the brilliant light all around Him was like that of a rainbow in a cloud on a rainy day. This was the appearance of the likeness of the glory of the LORD. And when I saw it, I fell facedown and heard a voice speaking.

WORSHIP EXPRESSION

This song was born out of a devotional time. After reading my Word and prayer, I waited for the Lord to speak. He wasn't coming like our typical exchange; thus, I began to say what my heart said. Then the Spirit took over, and the fire entered the room, and I was in worship for hours to the point I lost track of time and ended up being in that place for over five hours. I received great strength that day. For the Lord had given me directions to do something, but my flesh was weak. I needed the Lord to supersede my flesh that I carry out what He had directed just as spoken. May the Lord activate you to hear what He will have you do to overcome the world.

SELF-EVALUATION

1. Have you sought the Lord for strength?
2. If you asked, did you wait for how He would deposit your strength, or did you move right along?
3. What do you hear now?

PRAYER

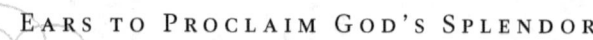

Ears to Proclaim God's Splendor

Dear Heavenly Father, over the entire world and the lover of our living soul. Lord, You have forgiven us more than we deserve. Thank You for the new season, where we are reminded of all that You have created. Thank You for Your song of strength, direction, and deposit of things we had no clue were within us. Lord, it is just a simple thank You. There are not enough words for all you have done, doing, and will do. We speak all these things in Jesus' holy name, I pray. Amen.

REFLECTION:

Heareth

EARS TO PROCLAIM GOD'S SPLENDOR

AFFIRMATION:

Revelation 21:6 (BSB)

And He told me, "It is done! I am the Alpha and the Omega, the Beginning and the End. To the thirsty I will give freely from the spring of the water of life.

PROCLAMATIONS:

Ezekiel 3:12

Then the spirit took me up, and I heard behind me a voice of a great rushing, saying, Blessed be the glory of the LORD from his place.

Activations: Song Twenty-Four
Bow Down & Worship

I bow down & worship at His feet
Just you and me, Lord

Bow down and worship at His feet
Here are my hands
Here are my feet
Here is my body
Cleanse me

I bow down & worship at His feet
Just you and me, Lord

Here is my heart
Here is my mind
Here is my soul Lord
Take Control

Bow down and worship at His feet
Here are my hands
Here are my feet
Here is my body
Use Me

SCRIPTURE SUPPORT

Bow Down

Matthew 4:9

And saith unto him, All these things will I give thee, if thou wilt fall down and worship me.

Spiritual Hope
Matthew 4:10 (BSB)

"Away from me, Satan!" Jesus declared. "For it is written: 'Worship the Lord your God and serve Him only.'

Lord Giveth
1 Samuel 2:7

The LORD maketh poor, and maketh rich: he bringeth low, and lifteth up.

WORSHIP EXPRESSION

I was astonished after finishing my prayer when the Lord delivered a prophetic song of worship. I was lying on the floor in my kitchen with the heavy glory lying on top of me. All I could do was cry and worship. As I worshipped, this song began to come from my belly. As I sang the song, I felt fire all over me. I ended up being on the floor for over an hour. When I finally came back to myself and stopped crying. I began to hear the Lord give me my next directions for my next season. Hearing from the Lord is very important. If we don't hear from God, can we truly say we are His people? Remember, the Lord said that His sheep know His voice. You know His voice because you are in a relationship aboard the ship of the Lord, allowing Him to take you down His stream and rivers that you will see all that He has in store for you.

Ears to Proclaim God's Splendor

SELF-EVALUATION

1. Are you on board the ship of the Lord?
2. Can you hear His all-aboard call?
3. What song of the Lord are you hearing?

PRAYER

Dear Heavenly Father, the Father of all things, thank You for allowing us the opportunity to get aboard your ship. Thank You for giving us access to deeper streams and rivers that will improve our life. Lord God activate us to hear your call to onboard the ship You have for us as we go from strength to strength and pillar to post. Lord release a song of direction in Jesus' holy name, I pray. Amen.

REFLECTION:

_____

_____

_____

_____

_____

_____

_____

Heareth

Ears to Proclaim God's Splendor

AFFIRMATION:

Psalm 113:7

He raiseth up the poor out of the dust, and lifteth the needy out of the dunghill;

PROCLAMATIONS:

Psalm 72:11
Yea, all kings shall fall down before him: all nations shall serve him.

Activation: Song Twenty-Five
Mark me with your burn

Lord send Your fire
Send it today
We need your fire
To cleanse us today
Burn our heart
That we may see
Just how great you are to me
Burn my mind
That I may think as you
Burn my ears
That I may hear you
Burn me, Lord
Burn me
That I may be what you called me to be
Burn me, Lord
Burn me
That all will see that I am with thee

SCRIPTURE SUPPORT

Fire
1 Corinthians 3:13 (NIV)

Their work will be shown for what it is, because the Day will bring it to light. It will be revealed with fire, and the fire will test the quality of each person's work.

Baptized by Fire
Matthew 3:11

I indeed baptize you with water unto repentance: but he that cometh after me is mightier than I, whose shoes I am not worthy to bear: he shall baptize you with the Holy Ghost, and with fire:

Refined Fire
1 Peter 1:7

So that the authenticity of your faith--more precious than gold, which perishes even though refined by fire--may result in praise, glory, and honor at the revelation of Jesus Christ.

WORSHIP EXPRESSION

After I had finished teaching, this song came down in a fire. The Lord brought down His delivering power in the form of fire. The manifestation happened on a prayer call a few years ago; God's fire touched everyone on the prayer call as I sang fire in their ears, mouth, and eyes. I couldn't say anything else but the song for several hours, even after the call. The Lord touched all of us by fire. His fire engulfed me for the remainder of the day. The issues I was having with warfare burned away. The struggle of being attacked in my mind burned away. Things attacking me on my job burned away. The fire of the Lord touched me on that day, and it was released through this song. Can you feel the fire?

SELF-EVALUATION

1. Has fire touched you?

Ears to Proclaim God's Splendor

2. Have you asked the Lord for His fire?
3. Did the Lord give you a song of fire?

PRAYER

Dear Heavenly Father, we need You. Lord, we need Your purifying fire to come into our hearts, minds, and bodies. We can see the new you have for us. Help us go out of the old places and walk into the new doors you have opened for us. Close every old door that nothing from behind may come to cause an issue in the new location. Lord, touch us now. One-touch that we will know of a new way in which you can move upon us. Fill our mouths with fire that breaks others free and ourselves. Lord send your fire. We ask all these things in Jesus' holy name, I pray. Amen.

REFLECTION:

Heareth

AFFIRMATION:

Luke 3:16 (BSB)

John answered all of them: "I baptize you with water, but One more powerful than I will come, the straps of whose sandals I am not worthy to untie. He will baptize you with the Holy Spirit and with fire.

PROCLAMATIONS:

Acts 11:16 (BSB)

Then I remembered the word of the Lord, as He used to say, 'John baptized with water, but you will be baptized with the Holy Spirit.'

LESSON 6

Hearing

*T*HE WORD HEARING MEANS the process, function, or power of perceiving sound. The focus of this lesson is the process of hearing. Suppose you are in a hurry, that is not going to work. If you are a talker, it's not going to work. Within the process of hearing, you must be still, quiet, and longing to hear your Lord's voice. Patient as you learn how you and He communicate. Just because you read the ways He talks to me may not be the way He speaks to you. Please don't limit yourself only to my processes but find your method. There is nothing in this world the Lord can't talk through. We know that because He used a donkey to speak in the Bible (Numbers 22:28-30). Therefore, take time to allow the Lord to show you the form of communication He uses for you to go forward.

SCRIPTURES TO MEDITATE ON HEARING

1. Job 42:5
    a. I have heard of thee by the hearing of the ear: but now mine eye seeth thee.

2. Proverb 20:12
    a. The hearing ear, and the seeing eye, the Lord hath made even both of them.

3. Mathew 13:13
    a. Therefore speak I to them in parables: because they see not; and hearing they hear not, neither do they understand.

4. Luke 2:46
    a. And it came to pass, that after three days they found him in the temple, sitting among the doctors, both hearing them, and asking them questions.

5. Acts 9:7
    a. And the men which journeyed with him stood speechless, hearing a voice, but seeing no man.

6. 1 Corinthians 12:17
    a. If the whole body were an eye, where were the hearing? If the whole were hearing, where were the smelling?

7. Galatians 3:2
    a. This only would I learn of you, Received ye the Spirit by the works of the law, or by the hearing of faith?

8. Galatians 3:5

a. Therefore, that ministereth to you the Spirit, and worketh miracles among you, doeth he it by the works of the law, or by the hearing of faith?

Activations: Song Twenty-Six
Crush-It, Jesus

Crussh it, Jesus
Crush it, Jesus
Crush it, Jesus
Crush
Crush
Crush

He can do it
Yes He can
He can do it
Yes He can
Yes He can
Yes He can
Yes He can

No More Pain
No More Sorrow
Crush
Crush
Crush

Crussh it, Jesus
Crush it, Jesus

Crush it, Jesus
Crush
Crush
Crush

No More Pain
No More Sorrow
Crush
Crush
Crush

He can do it
Yes He can
He can do it
Yes He can
Yes He can
Yes He can
Yes He can

SCRIPTURE SUPPORT

<u>Hammer</u>
Jeremiah 23:29
"Is not my word like fire, declares the LORD," and like a hammer that breaks a rock in pieces?

<u>Destroy Arguments</u>
2 Corinthians 10:5 (KJV)

Casting down imaginations, and every high thing that exalteth itself against the knowledge of God, and bringing into captivity every thought to the obedience of Christ;

2 Corinthians 10:5 (ESV)
We destroy arguments and every lofty opinion raised against the knowledge of God and take every thought captive to obey Christ,

<u>Guard</u>

Philippians 4:7 (KJV)
And the peace of God, which passeth all understanding, shall keep your hearts and minds through Christ Jesus.

Philippians 4:7 (ESV)
And the peace of God, which surpasses all understanding, will guard your hearts and your minds in Christ Jesus.

WORSHIP EXPRESSION

When I tell you the Lord will deliver you a song on demand, He did just that with this song. While preparing for my 'Soaring Wing Symposium: 2020', the Lord had given me the Scripture to act out. I didn't have a song for the Scripture at the time of teaching as I was using the song as an act of movement; however, I was faithful in knowing that the Lord would provide, and He did just that. As I read Jeremiah 23:29, I heard the above song used to help the people break down any items hindering from progress. The Lord began to tell us to ask Him to crush our issues; thus, that is what we did with the help of our Lord and Savior Jesus.

SELF-EVALUATION

1. Did you call on the hammer of the Lord to crush what was hindering you?
2. Have you asked the Lord for His fire to come and burn what can't be crushed?
3. Did you ask the Lord to give you your song of deliverance and protection?

PRAYER

Dear Heavenly Father, the Creator of all things, Lord send Your delivering hammer unto us to break us free from the enemy's reigns. We ask all these things in Jesus' holy name, I pray. Amen.

REFLECTION:

_____
_____
_____
_____
_____
_____
_____
_____

Ears to Proclaim God's Splendor

AFFIRMATION:

Isaiah 26:3 (BSB)
You will keep in perfect peace the steadfast of mind because he trusts in You.

Ears to Proclaim God's Splendor

PROCLAMATIONS:

John 14:27 (BSB)

Peace I leave with you; My peace I give to you. I do not give to you as the world gives. Do not let your hearts be troubled; do not be afraid.

Activations: Song Twenty-Seven
Greater is He

Greater Is He
Living in me
Greater is He
Living in me
Then he in this world

Above everything
OOH -OOH
He is our King
Greater is He living in me
Then he in this world

Greater Is He
Living in me
Greater is He living in me
Then he in this world

Above everything
He is King
Greater is He living in me
Then he in this world

Oh Oh Oh
Oh Oh OH

SCRIPTURE SUPPORT

Greater is God

1 John 4:4

Ye are of God, little children, and have overcome them: because greater is he that is in you, than he that is in the world.

Advocate

1 John 3:20

If our hearts condemn us, God is greater than our hearts, and He knows all things.

Overcome

1 John 5:4 (BSB)

because everyone born of God overcomes the world. And this is the victory that has overcome the world: our faith.

WORSHIP EXPRESSION

While walking into the church, I heard this song as soon as I stepped foot into the sanctuary. The music sounded like a thousand angels were singing, reminding me of the greatness of the Lord. As I looked around, no one else could hear the song. I began to pray, and that was the song the Lord wanted to be declared on that day. The Lord loves to drop new and refreshing songs to shift the atmosphere from one position to another. May your ears hear every song given good or warning that you will be in the right place to receive what the Lord has for you, for there is nothing more significant than our God.

SELF-EVALUATION

Hearing

1. How great do you believe our Lord is?
2. Do you have faith that He wishes to prosper and not harm you?
3. Do you hear your song of admiration?

PRAYER'

Dear Heavenly Father, the Lord worthy of all worship from everything that has breath. The Lord is worthy of all the praise. Lord, we adore You, for there is none more significant than You. Thank You for never leaving or forsaking us. Thank You for slaying all our enemies that we may occupy the land promised unto us. Lord, help us to hear praise that glorifies Your name for the great I AM that You are. Thank You for the newfound understanding and wisdom to represent You in all our ways. For without You, nothing is impossible, but with You, all things are possible. We ask all these things in Jesus' holy name. Amen.

REFLECTION:

_____

_____

_____

_____

_____

_____

Ears to Proclaim God's Splendor

AFFIRMATION:

Romans 8:31 (BSB)
What then shall we say in response to these things? If God is for us, who can be against us?

Ears to Proclaim God's Splendor

PROCLAMATIONS:

1 Kings 8:57 (BSB)
May the LORD our God be with us, as He was with our fathers. May He never leave us or forsake us.

Activation: Song Twenty-Eight
Greater is Coming

Greater is coming
Greater is coming
The Greater
The Greater
The greater is coming

He shall come in like the wind
Only those prepared will see Him
The greater
The greater is coming

Greater is coming
Greater is coming
The Greater
The Greater
The greater is coming

SCRIPTURE SUPPORT

Lord Overflow
1 Timothy 1:14
And the grace of our Lord was exceedingly abundant with faith and love, which is in Christ Jesus.

Redemption
Luke 21:28

And when these things begin to come to pass, then look up, and lift up your heads; for your redemption draweth nigh.

Perfected
1 John 2:5
But whoso keepeth his word, in him verily is the love of God perfected: hereby know we that we are in him.

WORSHIP EXPRESSION

This song was like an alarm clock waking me up one summer morning. I thought I left the radio on but knew I had not because there is no radio in my room unless it had come on my computer or phone. However, even after I awoke, the words continue to play over and over again. Until I spoke out of my mouth, "Lord, what greater thing is coming." Like the rushing wind, I began to hear the Lord tell me about things that were to come. The things He said to me were not concerning my ministry but the body of Christ. I wrote the points down and prayed over them for days until the burden broke.

Sometimes songs come to get you to intercede for someone or something. However, if I didn't have ears to hear, I would have missed two great opportunities to listen to the Lord in a new way and to intercede for the body of Christ. It wasn't long after that the Lord came again the same way with a new song, and that is when I learned the Lord used music to get my attention.

SELF-EVALUATION

Hearing

1. What does the Lord use to get your attention?
2. Have you heard Him tell you things concerning what is to come?
3. Did you hear something new while studying this song?

PRAYER

Dear Heavenly Father, the Lord that goes through the Earth day and night protecting us all people. The Lord helps us to have good faith, love, and perseverance within our lives. The Lord that loves us despite all things, for He is married to the backslider. Lord, help us to hear from You when you're getting our attention. Please help us understand why You are seeking us out and not get carried away in the how but in the what. Most of all, allow us to have ears to hear You in every way You desire. We ask all these things in Jesus' holy name, I pray. Amen.

REFLECTION:

_____
_____
_____
_____
_____
_____

Ears to Proclaim God's Splendor

AFFIRMATION:

2 John 1:6

And this is love that we walk according to His commandments. This is the very commandment you have heard from the beginning that you must walk in love.

EARS TO PROCLAIM GOD'S SPLENDOR

PROCLAMATIONS:

2 Timothy 2:22 (BSB)

Flee from youthful passions and pursue righteousness, faith, love, and peace, along with those who call on the Lord out of a pure heart.

Activation: Song Twenty-Nine
I Will Trust

I will Trust the Lord
I will Trust the Lord
I will Trust the Lord
On high
I will Trust the Lord
I will Trust the Lord
I will Trust the Lord
On High
I will Trust the Lord
I will Trust the Lord
I will Trust the Lord
On High

SCRIPTURE SUPPORT

Trust
Proverbs 3:5
Trust in the LORD with all thine heart, and lean not unto thine own understanding.

Instruction
Proverbs 22:19 (NKJV)
So that your trust may be in the LORD, I have instructed you today, even you.

Restraint

Ears to Proclaim God's Splendor

Proverbs 23:4 (BSB)

Do not wear yourself out to get rich; be wise enough to restrain yourself.

WORSHIP EXPRESSION

Trusting in the Lord can be difficult, especially when everything around you says the opposite of what the Lord has spoken. This song is one of those that came because I was having issues trusting. I was ready to give up, and with tears in my eyes, I told the Lord I was done. I asked Him why do people that are supposed to help always hurt? Why do people hide behind His name, saying they are doing things in His name, but really, they are just trying to control or see what they can get out of you? I told Him that He might as well put me back in the world because I had enough and didn't understand how He could love people. As I sat, I felt the fire of God on my back, and I became a stiff neck, so I got what I deserved. The power of God came into the room, and fell to the floor; and next the thing I remember is crying out, yes Lord, and my heart began to burn. The Lord was not going to allow the world circumstance to turn my heart to stone. When I was a child, I was called rock because I could become so stiff no one could move me. However, the Lord delivered me from that when I became a follower, and He was not about to allow me to go backward. Thus, this song became a song of major deliverance from people and hardship.

SELF-EVALUATION

1. Do you have issues of life that are blocking your hearing?

Hearing

2. Are you ready to allow the Lord to deliver you?
3. Can you hear your song of deliverance?

PRAYER

Dear Heavenly Father, thank You for not leaving us in our brokenness. Thank You for loving us more than we could ever love You. Lord, deliver us from the cares of this life and people. Help us to have a heart of flesh and not of stone. Lord, come and destroy every law in our heart that is against Your will. Help us to love the unlovable, for we were once unlovable. Lord, help us hear You beyond all the pain and hurt that we can find ourselves back to You as a willing vessel ready to be used for Your glory. We ask all these things in Jesus' holy name, I pray. Amen.

REFLECTION:

_____

_____

_____

_____

_____

_____

_____

_____

Ears to Proclaim God's Splendor

AFFIRMATION:

Proverbs 28:26 (BSB)

He who trusts in himself is a fool, but one who walks in wisdom will be safe.

PROCLAMATIONS:

Psalm 37:3 (BSB)

Trust in the LORD and do good; dwell in the land and cultivate faithfulness.

Activation: Song Thirty
One-Touch

Just one touch from the King
Will relieve us from everything
We just need
We just need
One-touch

Just one touch from the King
Will free us of everything
We just need
We just need
One-touch

One-touch of Grace
Right within the space
That nothing would be void
Because we are covered with his joy
We just need
We just need
One-touch

Just one touch from the King
Will relieve us from everything
We just need
We just need
one touch
From the King

SCRIPTURE SUPPORT

One-Touch
Mark 1:41 (BSB)
Moved with compassion, Jesus reached out His hand and touched the man. "I am willing," He said. "Be clean!"

Authority
Mark 4:39
And he arose, and rebuked the wind, and said unto the sea, Peace, be still. And the wind ceased, and there was a great calm.

Hope
Mark 5:41
And he took the damsel by the hand, and said unto her, Talitha cumi; which is, being interpreted, Damsel, I say unto thee, arise.

Ephesians 1:7
In whom we have redemption through his blood, the forgiveness of sins, according to the riches of his grace.

WORSHIP EXPRESSION

I was feeling invisible and unwanted. It is true when you hear prophets say they have high highs and low lows. A low moment for me internally, I was feeling unvalued and unloved. I studied God's Word on the topics and worshipped. However, the mood became worse, and I felt withdrawn. It was like seeing myself with no control. I knew it was not of God. As the

Hearing

Scripture says, when you have done all you can do, stand. Thus I stood in worship. I was singing until the Lord came. Boy, did He come! He came with a vengeance against the enemy, and it was as if I was there watching the battle between the Lord and the principality that had attacked me. I could hear the sword banging and the screams within the struggle.

I had been caught up in a vision and had no clue until I saw a creature that looked like an eagle at first, but I noticed something off because it had skinny legs. I was like, that is an owl disguised as an eagle. As soon as I said it, a warring angel fell from the heavens in front of me with a brown bag. He was not large but small; however, the enemy ran from him. The angel helped me up because I was sprawled out on the ground. Then I was taken into another vision that you will have to read about in my next book. Lol.

My point is a prophetic song. Don't just let yourself hear but ask God to give you access because you are exercising your authority as an ambassador in this world but not of it.

SELF-EVALUATION

1. Have you ever received a prophetic song that gave you access to visions?
2. Are you desperate to see Him in new ways?
3. Do you believe there are things God can show you beyond your understanding?
4. Have you asked Him to reveal the mysteries of His kingdom?

EARS TO PROCLAIM GOD'S SPLENDOR

PRAYER

Dear Father God, the Creator, lover, and protector of all things, we are open to every aspect of You. For You are the Holy One (Mark 1:24), we come today laying at Your feet asking You yet again to be the rock of our salvation (1 Cor 10:4). Help us trust You and walk in the right motives that we will receive when we ask because we are not asking amiss. We are not coming to ask for things that will bring pleasure unto ourselves, but we ask for Your wisdom and understanding. Open our ears to hear not just of this world but unto your Heaven that we will be open unto new realms and dimensions that will bring greater glory unto You on this Earth in Jesus' holy name, I pray. Amen.

REFLECTION:

_____

_____

_____

_____

_____

_____

_____

Hearing

EARS TO PROCLAIM GOD'S SPLENDOR

AFFIRMATION:

Psalm 33:9

For he spake, and it was done; he commanded, and it stood fast.

Hearing

PROCLAMATIONS:

Psalm 147:18 (BSB)

He sends forth His word and melts them; He unleashes His winds, and the waters flow.

Psalm 148:5 (BSB)

Let them praise the name of the LORD, for He gave the command, and they were created.

Lamentations 3:37 (BSB)

Who has spoken, and it came to pass unless the Lord has ordained it?

Ears to Proclaim God's Splendor

LESSON 7

Hearken

THE WORD HEARKEN MEANS to give respectful attention.², Which means to heed to what you hear. Most hear, but because you haven't trained yourself, you ignore or tune out what you hear because you mentally decide what is or isn't essential. When it comes to hearing from the Lord, everything He speaks is of importance. Get used to having notebooks with you that nothing is missed. Even if you don't understand, you still will have the information to review, or when praying and fasting, ask the Lord to give the story more clearly to you. However, remember some messages you will get right away, and some will take more time figuring out just as things are in the Word of God.

Please receive what you hear; accept it if you don't understand what you have heard. You may find yourself doing the opposite of those around you, and it may seem to cause warfare, and naturally, you want to fit in and don't want to be the odd man out. However, remember if the Lord said for you to go the way you are going, you need to follow the Lord. For the Lord knows what He has in store for you. If you hear nothing else, we must hearken to the Lord. You want the miracles, then hearken. It would be best if you learned to obey the small things you hear that will give you more incredible things beyond your wildest dream.

SCRIPTURES TO MEDITATE ON HEARKEN

1. Deuteronomy 15:5
   a. Only if thou carefully hearken unto the voice of the Lord thy God, to observe to do all these commandments which I command thee this day.

2. Jeremiah 17:24
   a. And it shall come to pass if ye diligently hearken unto me, saith the Lord, to bring in no burden through the gates of this city on the sabbath day, but hallow the sabbath day, to do no work therein;

3. Deuteronomy 15:15
   a. And thou shalt remember that thou was a bondman in the land of Egypt, and the Lord, thy God, redeemed thee: therefore I command thee this thing today.

4. 1 Samuel 15:22
   a. And Samuel said, Hath the Lord as great delight in burnt offerings and sacrifices, as in obeying the voice of the Lord? Behold, to obey is better than sacrifice, and to hearken than the fat of rams.

5. Isaiah 55:2

    a. Wherefore do ye spend money for that which is not bread? And your labor for that which satisfieth not? Hearken diligently unto me, and eat ye that which is good, and let your soul delight itself in fatness.

6. Daniel 9:19

    a. O Lord, hear; O Lord, forgive; O Lord, hearken and do; defer not, for thine own sake, O my God: for thy city and thy people are called by thy name.

7. Acts 4:19

    a. But Peter and John answered and said unto them, Whether it be right in the sight of God to hearken unto you more than unto God, judge ye.

Activations : Song Thirty-One
I Will

I Will
Bless the Lord
I Will
Bless the Lord
I Will
Bless the Lord
On high

I Will
Bless the Lord
I Will
Bless the Lord

I Will
Bless the Lord
On high

I Will
Bless the Lord
I Will
Bless the Lord
I Will
Bless the Lord
On high

SCRIPTURE SUPPORT

Blessings
Psalms 68:9 (NKJV)

Blessed be the Lord, who daily loaded us with benefits, even the God of our salvation. Selah

Messiah
Daniel 9:25

Know therefore and understand that from the going forth of the commandment to restore and to build Jerusalem unto the Messiah the Prince, shall be seven weeks, and threescore and two weeks: the street shall be built again, and the wall, even in troublesome times.

Restoration
Psalm 51:12

Restore unto me the joy of thy salvation; and uphold me with thy free spirit.

WORSHIP EXPRESSION

There are times when your spirit calls out to worship the Lord. This song came out of one of those times. Sitting and thinking of the goodness of God and how grateful I was for at that moment, my mind was at peace. I wasn't worrying, nor was my mind running all over the place. I was merely reflecting on how peaceful I felt. As I thought about these things, I heard this song in the spirit, and I opened my mouth and released it within the earth. The more I sang the music, the more peace came into the room. The deeper my worship became, tears began to flow. Not of pain, worry, or unhappiness but out of the fact that I had been tormented within my mind for so long, and now I was free. I thought of nothing but how the Lord had sustained and built me even in a time of uncertainty, but I was in peace. The Lord will indeed keep you in perfect peace whose mind is stayed on Him (Isaiah 26:3).

No matter where you are in life, our minds need to be at peace. We need to clear our minds and allow the Lord's power to filtrate through our minds that we will not drive ourselves crazy. If your mind keeps going and going, how can you hear the small still voice leading and guiding you? How can you know when His presence is before you to show you hidden mysteries that would shift your life into new dimensions? I had learned this at that moment. I understood more than ever why my mind needed to be stilled. I understood why the enemy worked so hard to keep my mind racing that I would miss what the Lord was sending and doing for me—sending me directions that will shift me into my next. That which has established my family and I for more extraordinary Kingdom work.

SELF-EVALUATION

1. Are you at peace?
2. What are your thoughts focused on the goodness of God or you?
3. Do you trust the Lord?

PRAYER

Dear Heavenly Father, the God of peace and the lover of our soul, Oh, how we love You and Your ways. Oh, how we trust and depend on You to help us to be more like You. Lord, drown the noise that is keeping us from hearing Your voice. Lord, stop the demonic chatter and the busyness of my environment. Help us to receive peace and stillness that quiets our soul. Lord, we thank You for our new stability and comfort in Jesus' holy name, I pray. Amen.

REFLECTION:

_____

_____

_____

_____

_____

Hearken

Ears to Proclaim God's Splendor

AFFIRMATION:

Proverbs 16:3 (NIV)
Commit to the Lord whatever you do, and he will establish your plans.

PROCLAMATIONS:

Psalm 23:1-2 (NIV)
The Lord is my shepherd, I lack nothing. He makes me lie down in green pastures; he leads me beside quiet waters.

Activation: Song Thirty-Two
Secret Place

He that dwell
In the secret place
Shall abide in shadows
Of the Almighty God

I will say of the Lord
That you are my protector and shield
And you will forever walk with me
I will hold your hand, allowing you
Guide and heal me
That I may dwell with thee

For He that Dwell
In the secret place
Shall abide in shadows
Of the Almighty God

SCRIPTURE SUPPORT

Divine Overshadowing
Psalm 91:1
He that dwelleth in the secret place of the most Highest shall abide under the shadow of the Almighty.

Shield
Psalm 33:20

Our soul waiteth for the Lord: he is our help and our shield.

Fearlessness
Psalm 91:5
Thou shalt not be afraid for the terror by night; nor for the arrow that flieth by day

WORSHIP EXPRESSION

This song is one of the first ones I received supernaturally. I remember sitting on my bed, studying God's word, when I began to hear the sounds of horses galloping. I began to look around but didn't see anything. I then toned my ears in and could listen to the galloping louder and louder. Then I began to hear the word dwell. After I repeated the word, the song came roaring in my room like winds and knocked me down on my bed. I cried and listened. The song brought so much deliverance. At that time, I was having issues trusting because I was going through so many storms. The rejection was trying to set in; however, the Lord knew what I needed. He opened the windows of Heaven and allowed His divine music to engulf my room, and from that day on, I have never been the same.

To dwell with the Lord, take trust. The enemy may try to call you out of His safe place. He may even torment you with foolish words of speaking against you, but you must dwell with the Lord. You must not move. You must trust that the Lord will be your refuge, no matter what is before or around. Your feet will be planted firmly on the rock of your salvation. You shall not be moved.

Ears to Proclaim God's Splendor

SELF-EVALUATION

1. What did the song disclose to you about yourself?
2. Do you dwell within the shadows of the Almighty God?
3. What do you use as covering from this world and cares of life?

PRAYER

Dear Heavenly Father, the God of all things, the real way maker for His people, we thank You for always dwelling with us even when we are unloveable. For every good and perfect thing comes from You, Lord. Please help us to stay with You at all times not to be lured by the enemy out of safety. Lord, give us discernment to know when things are not of You. Lord, allow us to dwell with You that we may lead us unto all trues. We ask these things in Jesus' Holy Name, Amen.

REFLECTION:

_____

_____

_____

_____

_____

Hearken

EARS TO PROCLAIM GOD'S SPLENDOR

AFFIRMATION:

Psalm 91:11
For he shall give his angels charge over thee, to keep thee in all thy ways.

PROCLAMATIONS:

Psalm 91:13

Thou shalt tread upon the lion and adder: the young lion and the dragon shalt thou trample under feet.

Activation: Song Thirty-Three
Send Your Presence

Fall on me
Fall on me
Let your Presence –
Fall on me_

Fall on me
Fall on me
Let your Presence –
Fall on me_

Come and see me
Come and see me
Come and See
Let Your Presence
Come to see me_

Come and see me
Come and See
Let Your Presence
Come to see me_
Jesus please
Jesus please
Come and see me

I need thee
I need thee

Come and see me
Jesus please

SCRIPTURE SUPPORT

<u>Living Water</u>
John 4:10
Jesus answered and said unto her, if you knew the gift of God, and who it is that saidth to thee, Give me to drink; you would have asked Him, and He would have given you living water.

<u>Streams Water</u>
Song of Solomon 4:15 (BSB)
You are a garden spring, a well of flowing water streaming down from Lebanon.

<u>Springs of Water</u>
Isaiah 12:3 (BSB)
With Joy, you will draw water from the springs of salvation.

WORSHIP EXPRESSION

This song of activation came when I was about to teach. However, I was struggling with feeling the presence of the Lord. I began to ask the Lord to send His presence. Just like in the natural world, there is time you want to see the person who brings you the most comfort. Once you get to know the Lord intimately, you will want Him to come and see you all the time. I am a hog when it comes to time with the Lord. I could spend every day and every second with Him. I know that is not always possible because I still have a calling to accomplish. For the Lord reminds me all the time by saying don't waste time, for you have work to do.

SELF-EVALUATION

1. What did the song disclose to you about yourself?
2. Did you feel the presence of God as your heart agrees with His Word?
3. Have you hearkened unto Jesus Christ?

PRAYER

Dear Heavenly Father, the Father of all things, the lover and the ruler of all things, thank You for Your willingness to teach us all things and not leave us to our destruction. Thank You for Your mercy while You are teaching us. Thank You, Lord, for helping us as leaders to follow instruction and lead Your people according to Your teaching and not our own. Thank You for not striking our followers (and us) down when we as leaders give the wrong instruction or act out of our own emotions instead of calling on Your healing and delivering power in Jesus' holy name, I pray. Amen.

REFLECTION:

_____

_____

_____

Hearken

Ears to Proclaim God's Splendor

AFFIRMATION:

John 4:14 (BSB)

But whoever drinks the water I give him will never thirst. Indeed, the water I give him will never thirst. Indeed, the water I give him will become in him a fount of water springing up to eternal life.

_____

_____

_____

_____

_____

_____

_____

_____

_____

_____

_____

_____

_____

_____

_____

PROCLAMATIONS:

John 7:38 (BSB)
Whoever believes in Me, as the Scripture has said: Streams of living water will flow from within him.

Activation: Song Thirty-Four
Loose Your Favor

Loose my favor, Lord
That my promises be fulfilled
Loose my favor
That I can do your will

Loose your favor
Oh God
Loose Your favor
Oh God
Loose Your favor

Send your quake Lord
Send your shakes, Oh God
Loose the gates, Lord
That my promise may be fulfilled

Loose your favor
Oh God
Loose your favor
Oh God
Loose your favor

Loose your favor, Lord
That my promise be fulfilled

SCRIPTURE SUPPORT

Favor
Psalm 106:4
Remember me, O LORD, with the favor You have toward Your people. Oh, visit me with Your salvation,

Remember
Nehemiah 5:19
Think upon me, my God, for good, according to all that I have done for these people.

Restore
Psalm 85:1 (BSB)
You showed favor to Your land, O LORD; You restored Jacob from captivity.

Grant
Psalm 85:7 (BSB)
Show us Your loving devotion, O LORD, and grant us Your salvation.

Mercy
Psalm 119:132 (BSB)
Turn to me and show me mercy, as You do to those who love Your name.

WORSHIP EXPRESSION

The favor of the Lord is necessary for our walk. We must have child-like faith continuing to petition our Lord for our promises and reminding Him of His promises and that we need them. I had to be reminded of this while awaiting the Lord to move on my behalf in a business deal. I never do anything without consulting the Lord. For I look for the favor of the Lord to overtake me that I will walk in His divine favor and accomplish all He has promised. However, waiting sometimes can be challenging. To know what the Lord has in store but waiting for His timing. That was the lesson out of this song.

I had decided to move before the Lord had given me the okay on something He has told me would happen. Since He said it would happen, why not make it happen for myself? When the item didn't work out, I became depressed. While in prayer, I heard the Lord say, "wait, I say wait upon me." My favor is perfect with no pain or sorrow, but you must learn to stay after repenting for moving out of the Lord's will. I then began to hear this song. The Lord had sent the message to teach me that we pray, worship, and wait upon Him to release the favor; however, we don't do it for ourselves. It wasn't long after the song the Lord did move, and it was in my favor. That divine favor brought with it promotion and endorsement that blessed not just me but my entire family. Remember, favor is not fair; but it is in the timing of the Lord. Thus pray, praise, and wait that the divine favor will come and bring promises that will change your entire family.

SELF-EVALUATION

1. Do you wait on the favor of the Lord?

2. Do you ask the Lord question about the decision you make?
3. Are you praying, praising, and waiting for the perfect timing of the Lord, or are you making it happen for yourself?

PRAYER

Dear Heavenly Father, the lover of our soul, thank You for every good and perfect thing that has come from you. Lord, help us to wait upon You to make way for us. Please help us to build our relationship with You that You become our advisor about everything. Lord forgive us for every past moved done without you. Please lead us to all truth that's ordered before we were born within the earth. Lord, we thank You for every mercy and grace. I say all of these things in Your Son Jesus' name. Amen.

REFLECTION:

_____
_____
_____
_____
_____
_____

Ears to Proclaim God's Splendor

AFFIRMATION:

Job 42:10 (BSB)
After Job had prayed for his friends, the LORD restored his prosperity and doubled his former possessions.

Ears to Proclaim God's Splendor

PROCLAMATIONS:

Job 8:21 (NIV)
He will yet fill your mouth with laughter and your lips with a shout of joy.

Activation: Song Thirty-Five
Shake Yourself

Shake -Shake -Shake
Shake Yourself Loose
Shake Yourself Loose

Shake -Shake -Shake
Shake Yourself Loose
Shake Yourself Loose

Read your Word
Praise Your God
Worship Him
Shake Yourself Loose
Shake Yourself Loose

Shake -Shake -Shake
Shake Yourself Loose
Shake Yourself Loose

Obey God
Obey God
Shake Yourself Loose
Shake Yourself Loose
Only God Can Free You
Shake us Loose
Shake us Loose Lord

Shake – Shake – Shake
Shake us Loose Lord
Shake us Loose Lord

Shake -Shake -Shake
Shake us Loose Lord
Shake us Loose Lord

SCRIPTURE SUPPORT

<u>Shake Off</u>
Isaiah 52:2

Shake thyself from the dust; arise, and sit down, O Jerusalem: loose thyself from the bands of thy neck, O captive daughter of Zion.

<u>Freedom</u>
Zechariah 2:7 (BSB)

"Get up, O Zion! Escape, you who dwell with the Daughter of Babylon!"

<u>Arise</u>
Isaiah 60:1 (BSB)

Arise, shine, for your light has come, and the glory of the LORD rises upon you.

WORSHIP EXPRESSION

We suffer for the namesake of our Lord and Savior. However, sometimes when we suffer, the Lord will say to the devil,

"Enough is enough. Arise, my child, I have had enough," and the devil will not use you as a doormat. This song came out of one of these times. I had been under warfare for weeks; the devil was attacking every relationship, my business, and even in my dream. As I worshipped the Lord driving home, I heard the Lord say, "Shake it off and arise." Then the song came. As the music came and I sang, I could feel the chain being removed. Then all of a sudden, the Lord picked me up in the spirit and moved me to another position. After that day, the warfare stopped, and I could move freely on the path the Lord had placed me.

SELF-EVALUATION

1. Do you need to shake the reign of the enemy off?
2. Do you believe the Lord can deliver you out of the hands of the enemy?
3. What are you hearing from the Lord after reading and singing the song?

PRAYER

Dear Heavenly Father, I want to thank You for all You have done. You are worthy of all the praise and the honor, and I worship You, Lord. The glory belongs to You, allowing us to hear Your voice and feel Your presence. We are undeserving, our God and redeemer. For protecting, healing, and delivering that we accomplish every good and perfect thing set before us in Your Son Jesus name, I pray. Amen.

Ears to Proclaim God's Splendor

REFLECTION:

Hearken

Ears to Proclaim God's Splendor

AFFIRMATION:

Malachi 4:2 (BSB)

"But for you who fear My name, the sun of righteousness will rise with healing in its wings, and you will go out and leap like calves from the stall.

PROCLAMATIONS:

Matthew 5:16
Let your light so shine before men, that they may see your good works, and glorify your Father which is in heaven.

LESSON 8

Hearkeneth

THE FINAL LESSON FOR your spiritual activation may seem small because there are only two primary Scriptures, but I want to caution you this chapter is the most important. If you ever pay attention to God's Kingdom's operations, He is into small things. Most big things happen because the first small things were completed. At least those big things that are everlasting. The entire meaning of hearkeneth is to follow God. Do not sway to the left or right; only go the way the Lord has directed. Once you have full access to hearing, you are without the excuse of knowing. You can't come before the throne of the Lord and say I didn't know. He will tell you didn't know because you didn't listen or you didn't ask. (The ask part is another subject, stay tuned for the book on asking the Lord.) We must do what we have been directed in our lives, and those we are called to help depends on it. Don't be one of those who are on a path that appears to be right. They won't know the truth until they come before the Lord. Not because He didn't try to tell them but because they don't listen. Sometimes the devil can get us so twisted that even with all of the signs and wonders of the Lord, we can get distracted from the purposes of the Lord. If you don't do what

He commands, fast, and pray, you can lose yourself and point others down the wrong path.

Therefore, only share what the Lord has directed you to share. Never try to add to what He is giving you, and don't use what you hear to make yourself appear to be greater than the rest of us.

SCRIPTURES TO MEDITATE ON HEARKENETH

1. Proverb 1:33
    a. But whoso hearkeneth unto me shall dwell safely, and shall be quiet from fear of evil.

2. Proverb 12:15
    a. The way of a fool is right in his own eyes: but he that hearkeneth unto counsel is wise.

<u>Activations: Song Thirty-Six</u>
Matchless Savior

I give you all the Glory
I give you all the Praise
For you are the Matchless wonder
Glory is Thy name
Glory is Thy name

I give you all the Glory
I give you all the Praise
For you are the Matchless Glory

Ears to Proclaim God's Splendor

Glory is Thy name
Glory is Thy name

For you are the One
That set my heart free
For you are the One
That came and rescued me
For you are the One
Who paid it all for me?
Matchless Savior
What can I say
For you are the one for me
So, I give you all the Glory

I give you all the Glory
I give you all the Praise
For you are the Matchless wonder
Glory is Thy name
Glory is Thy name

I give you all the Glory
I give you all the Praise
For you are the Matchless Glory
Glory is Thy name
Glory is Thy name

Glory is Thy name
Glory is Thy name

Matchless Savior

Matchless Healer
Matchless Deliver
Glory is Thy name
Glory is Thy name

SCRIPTURE SUPPORT

<u>Follow</u>
Mark 4:35
And the same day, when the even was come, he saith unto them, Let us pass over unto the other side.

<u>Faith</u>
Luke 8:25 (BSB)
"Where is your faith?" He asked. Frightened and amazed, they asked one another, "Who is this? He commands even the winds and the water, and they obey Him!"

<u>Press to Hear</u>
Luke 5:1 (BSB)
On one occasion, while Jesus was standing by the Lake of Gennesaret with the crowd pressing in on Him to hear the word of God,

WORSHIP EXPRESSION

We serve a matchless God, and nothing is greater. After reflecting on some past prophetic words, I began to sit quietly. I was in shock at how the Lord had taken me from what looked like a defeated position unto a victorious spot in less than one day. I went to bed feeling defeated and woke up to a call of

Ears to Proclaim God's Splendor

victory. The Lord had moved in the night. The Lord even gave me a dream about the matter the next night, making sure I understood what he had done and why. When we depend on the Lord, He moves on our behalf, for the Lord can change the outcome in a twinkle of an eye.

SELF-EVALUATION

1. Have you encountered your matchless savior?
2. Do you believe He will give you victory over all things?
3. What are you hearing from the Lord after reading and singing the song?

PRAYER

Dear Heavenly Father, I thank You for being my redeemer that is alive and well. Thank You for the continued victories over and over again. Thank You for a more in-depth hearing within our ear, eyes, and all my physical senses within my body. Lord activate all gifts from the top of our head to the soul of our feet to be used for Your glory in Your Son Jesus' name I pray. Amen.

REFLECTION:

_____

_____

_____

Hearkeneth

EARS TO PROCLAIM GOD'S SPLENDOR

AFFIRMATION:

Psalm 18:46 (BSB)
The LORD lives! Blessed be my rock! And may the God of my salvation be exalted.

PROCLAMATIONS:

Jeremiah 50:34 (BSB)

Their Redeemer is strong; the LORD of Hosts is His name. He will fervently plead their case so that He may bring rest to the earth but turmoil to those who live in Babylon.

Activation: Song Thirty-Seven
For You Loved Me

I worship for Your Glory
I worship you for Your Honor
For you loved me

You hold me
You keep me

I worship for Your Glory
I worshipped you for Your Honor
I worship You
For You loved me

For you loved me
For you loved me
For you loved me

You hold me
You keep me
You hold me
You keep me

I worship for Your Glory
I worshipped You for Your Honor
I Worship You
For you loved me

SCRIPTURE SUPPORT

Keeper
Psalm 121:5

The LORD is thy keeper: the LORD is thy shade upon thy right hand.

Shield
Psalm 28:7

The LORD is my strength and my shield; my heart trusted in him, and I am helped: therefore, my heart greatly rejoiceth; and with my song will I praise him.

Savior
Psalm 109:31

For he shall stand at the right hand of the poor, to save him from those that condemn his soul.

WORSHIP EXPRESSION

Throughout these expressions within this book, I've discussed love for the Father; however, it's another thing when the Lord shows His love. Love from Heaven is pure and life-changing, overwhelming and assuring of in right standing with our Savior and King Jesus. During this song's release, pure love was poured upon me and helped me hear clearer than I ever had before. It was as if I received a heart washing internally from every expression of love received on this earth couldn't compare. His love captivates every motive, every law within our heart, and every thought ever thought and helps us to see them from the perspective of God. My ears heard purity as it wrapped itself upon me like a rag full of clean water that then rinsed out all the murky water that I could hear and see clearly. Teaching me not to express my love but ask the Lord to send His love. Like Isaiah, our brother reminds us in Isaiah 55:8-9 the Lord's ways and thoughts are higher than ours; therefore, to be taken higher, we must be showing higher ways. Allow the Lord to show you the more excellent way you birth unquenchable love that no one can deny.

SELF-EVALUATION

1. How important is the love of God to you?
2. Have you asked Him to pour His love upon you?
3. What are you hearing?

PRAYER

Dear Heavenly Father, the great I AM. Lord, thank You for every experience You have given us within our lives, for every good and perfect thing comes from You. Thank You for giving us experiences beyond this world that build hope, understanding, and desire to know more concerning You. Lord, pour Your pure love upon us now, and we are praying. Change our hearts, minds, and souls that we become more effective for Your Kingdom. Open our human senses to whatever is true, whatever is noble, whatever is right, whatever is pure, whatever is lovely and admirable, showing us the more excellent way praiseworthy unto You. Take our hearing deeper, Lord, in Your Son Jesus' name. Amen.

REFLECTION:

Ears to Proclaim God's Splendor

AFFIRMATION:

Psalm 18:2 (BSB)

The LORD is my rock, my fortress, and my deliverer. My God is my rock, in whom I take refuge, my shield, and the horn of my salvation, my stronghold.

EARS TO PROCLAIM GOD'S SPLENDOR

PROCLAMATIONS:

Psalm 43:2 (BSB)
For You are the God of my refuge. Why have You rejected me? Why must I walk in sorrow because of the enemy's oppression?

Psalm 59:17 (BSB)
To You, O my strength, I sing praises, for You, O God, are my fortress, my God of loving devotion.

Psalm 69:30 (BSB)
I will praise God's name in song and exalt Him with thanksgiving.

_____

_____

_____

_____

_____

_____

_____

_____

_____

Hearkeneth

Activation: Song Thirty-Eight
The Sound

The Sound
The Sound
Do you hear the Sound?
The Sound of Victory
The Sound of horses –
Galloping

Do you hear the Sound?
OH- OH- OH OOO
Do you hear the Sound?
OH- OH- OH OOO
Do you hear the Sound?
OH- OH- OH OOO
The Sound of Victory
The Sound of Victory
Do you hear the Sound?
The Sound of horses

Do you hear the Sound?
OH- OH- OH OOO
Do you hear the Sound?
OH- OH- OH OOO
Do you hear the Sound?
OH- OH- OH OOO

Sound of Victory

Do you hear the Sound?
The Sound of horses –
Galloping
Do you hear the Sound of the Defeated Enemy?
He is going to Surrender

Do you hear the Sound?
Sound of Victory
You have the Victory
Do you hear the Sound?

SCRIPTURE SUPPORT

Sound
Revelation 19:6 (BSB)
And I heard a sound like the roar of a great multitude, like the rushing of many waters, and like a mighty rumbling of thunder, crying out: "Hallelujah! For our Lord God, the Almighty, reigns.

Sound of the Almighty
Ezekiel 1:24
And when they went, I heard the noise of their wings, like the noise of great waters, as the voice of the Almighty, the voice of speech, as the noise of an host: when they stood, they let down their wings.

WORSHIP EXPRESSION

I was sitting in a quiet place like I like to do from time to time and began to hear horses galloping. I kept looking around, and then I just knew I heard in the spirit. I told the Lord, I'm here. I then began to listen to the song and heard the music played for the song. Before long, I was using my entire body to carry out the tune. The Lord informed me that I had obtained the victory, and He did so by giving me a song. It wasn't long after that time someone sent me a message saying they heard I had been given a great victory. The Lord wants to inform you what is taking place in the spiritual realm for you. However, your ear has to be open to hear what the Spirit of the Lord is saying. Our will must be submitted unto the Lord that we will not miss His will, which is perfect unto us all.

SELF-EVALUATION

1. What sound do you hear?
2. Do you know the difference between the sound of the Lord calling you and Him attacking your enemies?
3. What do you hear now?

PRAYER

Dear Heavenly Father, the Creator of all things, thank You for the sound that will bring confidence in what You are doing on our behalf. Let us hear Your sound in the Earth, in Heaven, and our lives. Let us not miss You. Allow our ears to be open to every word spoken unto us and for those who are in need of knowing You in Jesus' Holy Name, I pray. Amen.

REFLECTION:

Hearkeneth

Ears to Proclaim God's Splendor

AFFIRMATION:

Revelation 19:6

And I heard as it were the voice of a great multitude, and as the voice of many waters, and as the voice of mighty thunderings, saying, Alleluia: for the Lord God omnipotent reigneth.

EARS TO PROCLAIM GOD'S SPLENDOR

PROCLAMATIONS:

Ezekiel 40:17

Then he brought me into the outer court, and there were chambers and a pavement laid out all around the court. Thirty chambers faced the pavement,

Activation: Song Thirty-Nine
God is Big

My God is Big
My God is so Big
So Wonderful
You saved Me
You died for Me
You took Calvary

My God is Big
My God, He is Strong
My God, He is living
On His throne

We serve a Big God
He is fighting all our battles
We are Victorious
For there is Glory in His name
Our God is Big

The enemy is defeated
Because He died on Calvary
Our God is Big

Wonderful Counselor
Mighty Messiah
My God is Big

Never been Defeated
He is the One
Only undefeated one
Our God is Big

SCRIPTURE SUPPORT

Stronghold
Psalm 28:8
The LORD is the strength of His people, a stronghold of salvation for His anointed.

Acknowledgment
Proverb 3:6
In all thy ways acknowledge him, and he shall direct thy paths

Direction
Proverb 11:5
The righteousness of the blameless directs their path, but the wicked fall by their own wickedness.

WORSHIP EXPRESSION

I began to sing the song by the Holy Spirit that dwells within me. It reminded me how a walk with the Lord could change me from a broken, lost place unto a place of peace, protection, and strength. There is a time when the pain is too great, and no words can bring the comfort you need. Your mind is unable to come up with anything that can comfort you. However, a prophetic song from God will come in and break up anything that tried to graft itself to you that is not of God. It's not just that the words that have the power; it's the fact that you are using your mouth, which is your most significant weaponry. Proverbs 13:2 (BSB) says, "From the fruit of his lips, a man will enjoy good things, but the faithless desire is violence."

Allow your lips to confirm the words that your heart hears. Sometimes this acknowledgment is all that is needed to begin the process of healing, deliverance, or guidance. That small amount of light can illuminate what is hidden and take you on a new walk—a closer walk with the Lord allowing Him to be your friend that sticks closer than any brother.

SELF-EVALUATION

1. How big is God in your life?
2. Do you use your mouth weaponry for building up or tearing down?
3. Have you heard your sound? The sound that will set you free.

PRAYER

Dear Heavenly Father, the lover of my soul, the God that loved me when I didn't know how to love myself. The God that friended me when I was unfriendly. Lord, I love you. Thank you for the song of direction, acknowledgment, and comfort. You are my everything. Help me always to desire to come to you first before anything else. Allow my ears to hear the heavenly music that I will stay in tune with you and not of this world.

Ears to Proclaim God's Splendor

Lord, I want to thank You for all that You had done even when I didn't understand what You were doing. Thank you. I pray all of these things in your Son Jesus' name. Amen.

REFLECTION:

_____

_____

_____

_____

_____

_____

_____

_____

_____

_____

_____

_____

_____

_____

_____

Hearkeneth

Ears to Proclaim God's Splendor

AFFIRMATION:

2 Corinthians 1:4 (ESV)
Who comforts us in all our affliction so that we will be able to comfort those who are in any affliction with the comfort with which we ourselves are comforted by God.

PROCLAMATIONS:

Isaiah 41:10 (NKJV)

Fear not, for I am with you; be not dismayed, for I am your God; I will strengthen you, I will help you, I will uphold you with my righteous right hand.

Activation: Song Forty
Knock Out

God's going to Knock You Out
I said God's going to Knock You Out
He's Going to Knock You OUT

I said Enemy A - A
I said Enemy A - A
I said Enemy A - A
Listen Up!

God's going to Knock You Out
I said, God's going to Knock You Out
He's Going to Knock You OUT

Listen UP
I said Enemies A - A
I said Enemies A - A
I said Enemies A - A

God's going to Knock You Out
I said, God's going to Knock You Out
He's Going to Knock You OUT

GOD'S GOING TO KNOCK YOU OUT!

SCRIPTURE SUPPORT

God Our Strength
Psalm 46:1
God is our refuge and strength; a very present help in trouble.

Divine Helper
Psalm 46:2
Therefore, will not we fear, though the earth be removed, and though the mountains be carried into the midst of the sea;

Courage
Psalm 91:5
Thou shalt not be afraid for the terror by night; nor for the arrow that flieth by day;

WORSHIP EXPRESSION

After being told by a talebearer that I was discussed negatively, I simply said, "Lord, what are You going to do about this?" I then heard this song. I began to sing the song by the Holy Spirit that dwells within me. As I sang the song, I felt the blows. My body language began to take on the theme, my heart, and mind agreed. I began to air punch and kick. My tone in the song became aggressive. I had become a battle-ax in song. I was ramming the enemy with the worship of confidence that my God would destroy my enemy. I didn't just believe it with my heart but with every facet of my being. The Lord has become first, and I have humbled myself under His protection, and no terror by day or night will move me. I shall allow the Lord as I humbly hide in Him to knock out my enemy!

Ears to Proclaim God's Splendor

SELF-EVALUATION

1. What did you hear after singing or reading the song?
2. Do you believe in your heart that the Lord will destroy your enemies?
3. Do you hear how He will do it?
4. Are you allowing God to use you as weaponry?

PRAYER

Dear Heavenly Father, the lover of my soul, the God that protects me day and night. The God that gives me the victory over and over again against my enemies. Lord teach my voice how to war using the Word from Heaven to strike down my enemies and those who plot to do me harm and rise against me. The Lord, my Rock, train my body to war, moving within me that every part of me takes on the stance of victory for the battle has already been completed by my Lord and Savior, Jesus. The Lord is knocking down every demonic altar and every evil word spoken. Activate every part of me, Lord, to proclaim You throughout the land. I say all of these things in your Son Jesus' name. Amen.

REFLECTION:

_____

_____

_____

Hearkeneth

Ears to Proclaim God's Splendor

AFFIRMATION:

Psalm 112:7
He shall not be afraid of evil tidings: his heart is fixed, trusting in the Lord.

PROCLAMATIONS:

Psalm 112:8
His heart is established, he shall not be afraid until he sees his desire upon his enemies.

Conclusion

Hearing from the Lord is necessary to overcome this dark world and to lead you to the place the Lord has destined. We need our ears to listen to the voice of the Lord. His voice is prophecy so that we are not manipulated or lied to, and to hear the enemy attacks that we can send the armies of the Lord through our Savior Jesus Christ to fight out battles. I learned this information through the training of the Holy Spirit. He would awake me and say, what do you hear? Or when I would come into a room, He would ask me, "What do you hear?" When someone gave me a word, He would ask if I heard Him in the word. Training by the Holy Spirit taught me that the Lord has a sound that none can deny and that must be activated, taught, and trained to hear the sound that we would become the elite army the Lord has called His people to be in this world.

Even with making that statement, I have found that many five-fold leaders do not hear from the Lord. Thus they can not train the body to do what they have not experienced nor acknowledged. Leadership not being able to hear the Lord grieves me because how can one lead effectively without the guidance of who has called them. The Lord has continually shown me this weakness in the body of Christ; therefore, I must send out the call within this book that we will take heed and become trained that as the body of Christ, we can pass the learning down to His people who are called by His name. Using the activations in this book to ignite all called by the name Jesus Christ of Nazareth for we are in a war, and if you can not hear your orders, you will miss what battle position you are to stand.

Thus the download of this book came for that purpose and that purpose only for me to activate His people that they can be His people called by His name. We must get in a real relationship with the Lord. We can no longer have a form of Him. If we say we want Him to bless us, but we represent Him falsely, we become the cursed one because the Lord hates mockery. The people called by His name can no longer be unlearned or lack training and understanding. We must hear from the Lord because how can we effectively lead others if we had no clue of the direction the Lord is taking us. We can't take men's word as what God is saying, but we try every spirit by the spirit because we know the enemy can turn himself into the angel of light. However, when you usher in the glory of the Lord, nothing false, broken, or untrue can stay hidden, for the Lord will reveal every demonic agenda.

Therefore let us long to know the Lord in every way, hearing Him day and night that we will reach our divine purpose. While helping those called unto us get there as well. We are serving God and man just as our Lord and Savior did for us. For the Lord is calling us to do greater than the generals of faith before us. However, we must learn from the mistakes that we can accomplish more than what has already been completed. The only way we can do this is by simply listening to the Lord and allowing Him to lead us. There are many voices in the world; however, one that has never changed for truth is the voice of the Almighty God. Learn to hear, listen, and carry out. For you will be without excuse because of all the teachings that are available to us all. We must be willing to learn from one another. By merely trying the spirit by the spirit, but if you don't know God's nature, what will you try it by?

Here are encouraging words for the late and great Dr. Kathryn Kuhlman:

Kathryn Kuhlman – What Matters Most – Teaching at Oral Roberts University 1974. "I have failed because I sometimes listen to other voices. If I only knew what God had for me before, I would not have ruined the washes. I didn't do it initially; I didn't know. If I had only known. I did things out of ignorance. I did it out of not waiting for His(Holy Spirit) leading. I did it because I listen to other voices instead of his voice. There has never been a time I didn't want more than anything for the Lord to keep me as the apple of his eye (Kuhlman, 2020)."

About the Author

Zolisha L Ware is a married mother of three and a grandmother of nine adorable grandchildren. Her husband is Timothy Ware Sr., and they reside in Normal, IL. Before a relationship with the Lord, Zolisha was robbed of her education by anger and bitterness due to the life struggles of being a teenage mother. However, once she became under the healing power of Jesus Christ, the Spirit of the Lord directed Zolisha in 2007 to pursue her education. Shortly after the ushering of the Spirit of the Lord to get her education, Zolisha found out that she should have already received her high school diploma. However, since it was so many years after that period, Zolisha was required to take two online tests. One was an English examination and a Science examination to receive a fully accredited High School Diploma. I am glad to report she completed both tests online quickly. After completing the classes, Zolisha was awarded her High School diploma in September 2007 from Excel High School in Plymouth, MN.

Once she was able to accomplish her high school diploma, she was continually driven by the Spirit of the Lord to further her education by signing up for college. Therefore, in the spring of 2008, Zolisha began to attend Lincoln College located in Normal IL. She received her Associate's Degree in Arts in 2011, and three years later, she received her Bachelors in Liberal Arts. Once Zolisha obtained her Bachelor's Degree, she thought she had completed her studies. However, the drive for education continued to burn heavily within her. Therefore, after consulting with the Lord, she enrolled in Liberty University located in Lynchburg, VA, in August of 2014. A year or so after being registered within the Master's program in May of 2015, Zolisha encountered a supernatural dream that lasted for three nights. Zolisha was tested in the courts of heaven on things that the Lord had delivered her from within that dream, like greed, anger, sexual immorality, hate, and perversion.

At the end of that dream, Zolisha was given a mandate straight from heaven to birth, an outreach program geared toward helping women be more Christ-centered. Thus, Safe Haven Women Outreach (SHWO) was birthed. The program serviced the Bloomington-Normal, IL Community area. Safe Haven Women Outreach also had an online presence on Facebook. The program was said to bring God's deliverance power and transform every life that steps within the outreach program's thresholds.

Once the program was fully up and running, Zolisha continued to pursue her education with Liberty University, where she received a Master's degree in Executive Leadership in March of 2017. Shortly after finishing, Zolisha received a mandate from heaven, confirming she would no longer pursue secular education. Instead, she was to learn all she could concerning

About the Author

the Kingdom of God. Therefore, she enrolled in Anchor Theological Seminary and Bible Institute, where she finished with a Doctorate in Pastoral Theology in March of 2020. During her time in school, the Lord came to Zolisha by way of a vision in October of 2018 and told her she would be what Samuel was to Saul and what David was to Nathan, and she would have the authority of Ezekiel.

During this time, not only was Zolisha learning of God's word more deeply, but she was also learning the operation of the Holy Spirit in the demonstration. It wasn't long after being called into the office did the promises of the Lord show up in Zolisha by way of her operation in healing, deliverance, and miracles. Zolisha also began to have Angelic encounters where the angels of the Lord would give her insight into biblical facts that she is to write about to help bring a greater understanding of the Kingdom of God. Zolisha is grateful for this grace she has been given and understands that she must share everything, given that the people of God will have a greater understanding of biblical teaching. Zolisha believes that in God, learning never stops. She believes we all should be striving to have the mind of Christ by studying all we can to help us be more like Jesus. Therefore, her studies will continue until the Lord returns. She will continue to write what the angels, Holy Spirit give her until she has fulfilled her assignment.

Zolisha has featured on many platforms, including radio and podcast. She has also been on the cover of Rejoice Essential Magazine, highlighting her full launch into ministry. She is highly sought out as a prophetic teacher and Prophetess who leaves God's Glory wherever she teaches. You can find Dr. Zolisha L Ware by simply searching her name.

Contact Info:
Facebook//Instagram: Zolisha L Ware, Dr. Zolisha L Ware
Email: infozlware@gmail.com

Facebook//Instagram: Fearless Fire Network, Fearless Fire Women
Email: fearlessfirenetwork@gmail.com

Facebook: Fearless Transformation Center
Email: info@fearlesscenters.com

Website: www.fearlesscenters.com

Notes

Bibliography

(n.d), M.-W. (2020, November 27). Psalm. Retrieved from Merriam-Webster.com dictionary: https://www.merriam-webster.com/dictionary/psalm

(n.d., M.-W. (2019, March 26). Sustain. Retrieved from Merriam-Webster.com dictionary: https://www.merriam-webster.com/dictionary/sustain?utm_campaign=sd&utm_medium=serp&utm_source=jsonld

Kuhlman, D. K. (2020, December 20). What Matters Most. Tulsa, OK, USA. Retrieved from https://youtu.be/HKNqELlE17o

Merriam-Webster. (2020, 26 December). (n.d.). Heard. . Retrieved from Merriam-Webster.com dictionary: https://www.merriam-webster.com/dictionary/heard

Strong LL.D S.T.D, J. (1996). The New Strong's Complete Dictionary of Bible Words. Nashville, Tennessee: Thomas Nelson Publishers.

Thompson, F. C. (2007). Thomas and Chain Study Bible. Indianapolis, IN: B.Bkirkbride Bible Co. INC.

Index

A

abundance, 178
abundant life, 37
acceptance, 37, 102
access, 9, 14, 30, 77, 78, 99, 131, 194, 233, 274
accomplish, 49, 50, 85, 256, 262, 269, 312, 313
accomplished, 29, 49, 93
accountable, 154
acknowledge, 19, 298
activate, 4, 7, 23, 102, 111, 141, 148, 171, 187, 278, 311
Activate, 306
activated, 4, 99, 138, 148, 310
activation, 7, 12, 92, 111, 119, 132, 141, 148, 154, 161, 167, 255, 274
Activation, 4, 5, 22, 28, 35, 42, 48, 109, 118, 124, 130, 146, 152, 159, 165, 180, 186, 198, 219, 225, 231, 248, 254, 260, 267, 282, 290, 297, 304
activations, 5, 311
admirable, 284
admiration, 44, 65, 215

Index

adversary, 16
advise, 55
advisor, 263
Advocate, 68, 214
AFFIRMATION, 26, 33, 40, 46, 53, 68, 74, 81, 88, 95, 105, 114, 122, 128, 135, 144, 150, 157, 163, 169, 178, 184, 190, 196, 202, 211, 217, 223, 229, 236, 246, 252, 258, 265, 272, 280, 287, 295, 302, 308
affliction, 58, 60, 302
afraid, 13, 116, 249, 305, 308, 309
afresh, 173, 174
aggressive, 305
alive, 1, 278
Almighty, 4, 5, 6, 16, 248, 250, 291, 312
Alpha and Omega, 186
amazed, 277
ambassador, 233
Anchor, 159, 315
angelic voices, 4
angels, 77, 78, 132, 214, 252, 315
anointed, 95, 96, 298
appetite, 137
appointment, 93
armies, 310
armor of the Lord, 15
arrogance, 50
assignments, 133
assurance, 43, 65
atmosphere, 92, 214
attack, 2, 3, 4, 85

attacked, 160, 199, 233
attention, 4, 71, 85, 166, 220, 221, 239, 274
authority, 10, 233, 315
awaken, 2, 171

B

Bachelors, 314
balances, 55
battle, 60, 86, 233, 305, 306, 311
battles, 297, 310
beautiful, 4, 132, 166
beauty for ashes, 96
beginning, 7, 33, 59, 63, 92, 140, 186, 223
Beginning, 190
believe, 21, 43, 105, 106, 111, 139, 161, 176, 215, 233, 269, 278, 305, 306
belly of hell, 60
Bible, 1, 4, 8, 9, 13, 55, 56, 77, 99, 204, 315
birth, 110, 111, 126, 160, 284, 314
blessed, 5, 100, 109, 110, 111, 114, 140, 262
Blessed, 109, 114, 130, 146, 191, 242, 280
blessing, 77, 116
block, 13, 15, 77
blood, 2, 174, 182, 232
blood of Christ, 2
Bloomington-Normal, 314
blows, 305
body, 8, 29, 72, 91, 99, 101, 114, 116, 131, 132, 137, 138, 154, 185, 192, 205, 220, 278, 292, 305, 306, 310, 311

bondman, 240
bones, 17
book, 3, 7, 9, 11, 16, 56, 60, 71, 92, 137, 233, 274, 283, 311
bow, 147, 192
Bread of Life, 35, 36
breakthrough, 3, 126, 138
breath, 5, 43, 74, 215
bribe, 144
bride, 29, 173
brighter, 128
broken, 3, 17, 85, 148, 298, 311
brokenhearted, 95, 96
brokenness, 2, 3, 227
bullock, 16, 60
Burn, 198
business, 43, 64, 262, 269

C

Calling, 29
camp, 86
captives, 95, 96
captivity, 208, 261
cares of this life, 161, 227
carnal, 1, 14
carnality, 13
case, 78, 281
Casting down, 7, 208
category, 43, 65
chambers, 296

chastised, 60
checks, 55
child, 36, 125, 130, 226, 261, 269
children, 15, 18, 21, 60, 64, 69, 214
chill bumps, 43, 64
choice, 9, 10
Choose, 100, 101
chosen, 38, 101, 102
circumstance, 226
city, 58, 114, 240, 241
cleanse, 14, 23, 30, 44, 65, 79, 126, 138, 198
clear, 1, 9, 78, 119, 243
cloud, 11, 187
clue, 85, 102, 131, 160, 188, 233, 311
comfort, 5, 85, 96, 147, 244, 255, 298, 299, 302
command, 114, 116, 117, 237, 240
commandments, 50, 114, 116, 223, 240
commune, 167
communicate, 9, 56, 57, 72, 140, 141, 204
communication, 8, 13, 15, 56, 57, 72, 77, 92, 100, 141, 204
communion, 29
compassion, 232
complaining, 125
comprehend, 137
conceived, 110
condemn, 214, 283
confessed, 125
confident, 154
conquerors, 89
contaminates, 29

control, 2, 102, 159, 166, 226, 232
correction, 55, 154
counsel, 77, 99, 275
courts, 3, 4, 314
covenant, 19
creation, 9, 154
Creator, 23, 30, 154, 209, 234, 292
creature, 138, 233
cross, 14
crowns, 7
Crush, 206, 207
curse, 126
cycle of torcher, 181

D

darkness, 53, 63, 103, 128, 138
days, 4, 5, 62, 175, 205, 220
dead things, 2
declaration, 126
declare, 63, 81, 107, 125, 138, 181
decoding, 57
decree, 124, 125, 145
Defeated, 291, 298
deliver, 51, 78, 148, 208, 227, 269
deliverance, 2, 49, 92, 95, 126, 138, 147, 148, 181, 209, 226, 227, 249, 299, 314, 315
delivered, 147, 193, 226, 314
delivers, 140
demonic agenda, 311

demonic attacks, 154
demonic chatter, 244
demonstrate, 50, 138, 140
demystify, 9, 98
deny, 1, 154, 284, 310
deposit, 161, 187, 188
depressed, 262
depths, 37, 38
desire, 1, 7, 9, 14, 15, 16, 38, 72, 93, 98, 110, 119, 133, 137, 221, 284, 299, 309
destroy, 2, 9, 208, 227, 305, 306
devil, 55, 78, 83, 84, 111, 131, 154, 268, 269, 274
devotion, 178, 261, 288
devotional, 187
dimensions, 234, 243
direction, 14, 37, 65, 188, 194, 299, 311
directions, 12, 187, 193, 243
discernment, 250
dislikes, 8, 14
dismayed, 303
disobedience, 85
distracted, 274
divine, 10, 23, 37, 44, 65, 86, 249, 262, 311
Divinity, 11
doer, 98, 100
dominion, 151
doors, 14, 200
double-mindedness, 2
dream, 131, 171, 240, 269, 278, 314
dreaming, 132

dreams, 8
dwell, 5, 15, 23, 30, 44, 65, 102, 119, 153, 230, 248, 249, 250, 268, 275

E

eagle, 233
ear gate, 4
ears, 4, 10, 15, 44, 78, 79, 85, 93, 99, 102, 132, 138, 148, 153, 154, 176, 198, 199, 214, 220, 221, 234, 249, 284, 292, 299, 310
earth, 8, 9, 11, 18, 19, 37, 49, 57, 59, 60, 61, 65, 98, 114, 116, 119, 125, 126, 141, 150, 243, 263, 281, 283, 305
east wind, 5
effective, 10, 284
electronic device, 11
embrace, 186
emotions, 57, 256
encoding, 57
encounters, 98, 99, 315
End, 190
endorsement, 262
enemies, 5, 9, 114, 215, 292, 306, 309
enemy, 2, 3, 4, 5, 50, 77, 85, 86, 91, 102, 160, 181, 182, 209, 233, 243, 249, 250, 269, 288, 297, 305, 310, 311
English, 137, 313
enjoy, 299
envious, 37
escape, 3
essential, 1, 11, 12, 239
establish, 58, 116, 125, 246

established, 20, 36, 56, 124, 125, 126, 244, 309
evangelists, 101
evil, 3, 5, 18, 106, 275, 306, 308
example, 14, 78
excuse, 274, 312
expectation, 7
expression, 50, 132, 175, 283
eye, 18, 59, 204, 205, 278, 312

F

facet, 8, 119, 305
faith, 10, 38, 62, 72, 77, 85, 153, 160, 180, 199, 205, 206, 214, 215, 219, 221, 224, 261, 277, 311
faithful, 62, 208
faithfulness, 17, 140, 230
familiar, 9
Father, 1, 11, 15, 23, 28, 29, 30, 36, 37, 44, 49, 51, 55, 56, 61, 63, 64, 65, 68, 72, 78, 86, 92, 102, 105, 106, 107, 110, 111, 119, 125, 126, 132, 141, 148, 154, 161, 167, 175, 176, 182, 188, 194, 200, 209, 215, 221, 227, 234, 244, 250, 256, 263, 269, 273, 278, 283, 284, 292, 299, 306
favor, 102, 260, 261, 262
fear, 5, 13, 15, 50, 86, 141, 272, 275, 305
fearful, 13
feet, 2, 36, 102, 119, 176, 192, 234, 249, 253, 278
fellowship, 8, 63, 147
Fight, 83, 84, 85
filthy, 37

fire, 10, 43, 58, 65, 86, 92, 132, 166, 175, 181, 187, 193, 198, 199, 200, 202, 207, 209, 226
flawed, 65
flesh, 4, 49, 50, 51, 56, 62, 125, 137, 138, 154, 187, 227
flood, 3
folly, 18
forever, 5, 6, 7, 58, 68, 99, 138, 248
forgive, 16, 179, 241, 263
forgiven, 18, 179, 188
forgiveness, 174, 232
formula, 125
fornicating, 37
forsake, 218
fortress, 287, 288
foundation, 107, 131
fountain, 75
free, 10, 92, 124, 165, 182, 200, 209, 231, 242, 243, 276, 299
freedom, 3
Frightened, 277
fruit of holiness, 38
fulfill, 8, 90, 103, 110, 119, 126
fulfillment, 92

G

gain, 1, 13, 14
garden, 10, 58, 255
gates,, 15, 260
gifts, 7, 102, 110, 278
gladness, 17, 125

glorified, 11, 96, 132

glorify, 11, 50, 147, 273

glory, 9, 49, 53, 55, 57, 71, 85, 92, 106, 107, 110, 111, 120, 132, 141, 167, 174, 175, 180, 186, 187, 191, 193, 199, 227, 234, 268, 269, 278, 311

Glory, 1, 2, 3, 6, 7, 8, 11, 22, 26, 28, 42, 48, 49, 118, 166, 173, 187, 275, 276, 277, 282, 297, 316

God, 1, 2, 3, 4, 5, 6, 8, 9, 10, 11, 12, 14, 15, 16, 17, 18, 19, 21, 23, 26, 27, 29, 30, 36, 37, 42, 43, 44, 49, 50, 53, 55, 56, 58, 59, 60, 62, 63, 64, 65, 71, 77, 84, 86, 88, 90, 91, 96, 100, 102, 109, 110, 111, 114, 116, 118, 119, 122, 123, 131, 138, 139, 140, 144, 146, 148, 153, 154, 155, 160, 163, 165, 166, 171, 172, 173, 175, 176, 180, 182, 184, 193, 199, 208, 214, 217, 218, 220, 226, 232, 233, 234, 239, 240, 241, 242, 243, 244, 248, 249, 250, 255, 256, 260, 261, 267, 269, 274, 277, 280, 284, 287, 288, 291, 295, 297, 298, 299, 302, 303, 304, 305, 306, 311, 312, 314, 315, 316

good treasure, 116

goodness, 5, 243, 244

govern, 56

government, 36

grace, 33, 49, 83, 85, 100, 153, 163, 174, 180, 219, 232, 263, 315

grasp, 99, 111

gratitude, 122

greater, 7, 8, 9, 14, 29, 37, 38, 69, 78, 92, 132, 140, 161, 167, 214, 219, 220, 234, 275, 277, 311, 315

grieves, 310

groans, 137

ground, 5, 114, 116, 233

guidance, 72, 299, 310

guilty, 125

H

Hallelujah, 35, 291
hammer, 207, 209
hands, 63, 175, 192, 269
hardship, 226
healing, 2, 49, 102, 126, 138, 181, 182, 256, 269, 272, 299, 313, 315
heals, 140
hear, 2, 3, 4, 5, 7, 8, 9, 11, 13, 15, 16, 17, 18, 19, 20, 21, 24, 30, 38, 44, 55, 65, 69, 72, 77, 79, 84, 85, 86, 91, 92, 93, 98, 102, 110, 111, 119, 124, 125, 126, 132, 133, 137, 138, 140, 141, 148, 150, 153, 154, 160, 161, 166, 167, 171, 175, 176, 181, 182,187, 193, 194, 198, 204, 205, 214, 215, 220, 221, 227, 232, 233, 234, 239, 240, 241, 243, 249, 262, 269, 275, 277, 283, 284, 290, 291, 292, 299, 306, 310, 311, 312
heard, 1, 3, 4, 8, 10, 11, 14, 20, 21, 55, 56, 57, 58, 59, 60, 61, 62, 63, 78, 85, 98, 99, 132, 138, 147, 160, 166, 171, 175, 187, 191, 204, 208, 214, 221, 223, 239, 243, 262, 269, 284, 291, 292, 295, 299, 305, 310
hearer, 98, 99, 100
heareth, 19, 171, 172, 173
Heareth, 171
hearing, 1, 7, 8, 9, 10, 11, 13, 14, 18, 55, 77, 78, 99, 132, 137, 138, 153, 154, 166, 181, 194, 204, 205, 206, 227, 239, 244, 269, 274, 278, 284, 311
hearken, 16, 19, 114, 116, 239, 240, 241
hearkeneth, 274, 275

heart, 7, 14, 15, 18, 29, 47, 56, 79, 125, 131, 147, 153, 154, 173, 175, 187, 192, 198, 224, 225, 226, 227, 256, 276, 283, 299, 305, 306, 308, 309

hearts, 53, 120, 141, 153, 157, 176, 200, 208, 214, 284

heaven, 2, 4, 11, 16, 24, 30, 78, 91, 116, 126, 131, 137, 151, 273, 314

Heaven, 3, 44, 65, 92, 161, 176, 182, 234, 249, 283, 292, 306

heavens, 3, 8, 10, 18, 26, 27, 35, 92, 101, 119, 233

Hebrew, 9

help, 13, 24, 29, 30, 38, 44, 56, 65, 72, 85, 90, 92, 93, 98, 102, 103, 126, 132, 141, 147, 155, 160, 161, 167, 208, 215, 221, 226, 227, 244, 249, 250, 263, 274, 303, 305, 315

High School Diploma, 313

hindering, 37, 208, 209

hindrance, 4, 13, 15

holy, 5, 6, 28, 29, 33, 116, 123, 138, 176, 182, 188, 194, 200, 209, 215, 221, 227, 234, 244, 256

Holy Ghost, 26, 147, 199

Holy Spirit, 2, 22, 30, 65, 102, 140, 147, 153, 160, 186, 202, 203, 298, 305, 310, 312, 315

honest, 125

honor, 7, 49, 138, 199, 269

Honor, 6, 7, 282

hope, 1, 40, 135, 147, 148, 159, 164, 178, 284

horrible pit, 36

hours, 4, 187, 199

humbly, 305

humility, 49, 131

hurt, 91, 226, 227

husband, 30, 175, 313

hymns, 153, 157

I

ideas, 57
identity, 30, 131
idol, 14
ignorance, 312
imparting, 79
impossible, 14, 215
increase, 38, 111, 114
infirmities, 180
influence, 2
influencers, 2
information, 1, 13, 57, 77, 98, 153, 166, 239, 310
inhabits, 3
inner court, 186
instructed, 131, 225
instruction, 2, 71, 256
instructions, 11, 12, 132
interceded, 137
invite, 15, 23, 29, 30
Isaiah, 3, 8, 18, 19, 36, 56, 59, 96, 140, 181, 211, 240, 243, 255, 268, 284, 303
isolated, 175
Israel, 9, 11, 16, 21, 81, 178
issues of life, 227

J

jealous, 111
Jesus, 1, 4, 15, 24, 26, 28, 29, 30, 33, 36, 37, 38, 44, 48, 51, 61, 63, 64, 65, 70, 72, 78, 79, 86, 90, 92, 93, 99, 102, 103, 110, 111, 120, 123, 126, 130, 131, 132, 133, 141, 148, 155, 160, 161, 163, 167, 172, 176, 180, 182, 188, 193, 194, 199, 200, 206, 207, 208, 209, 215, 219, 221, 227, 232, 234, 244, 250, 254, 255, 256, 263, 269, 277, 278, 283, 284, 292, 300, 306, 310, 311, 313, 315
Jordan, 15
journal, 11, 56
joy, 17, 22, 43, 69, 70, 78, 96, 231, 242, 266
judgment, 81, 96, 153

K

Kathryn Kuhlman, 312
Kindness, 165, 166
King, 5, 78, 118, 130, 139, 140, 146, 181, 213, 231, 283
Kingdom, 2, 8, 10, 14, 15, 49, 103, 133, 137, 155, 176, 244, 274, 284, 315
kingdom workers, 93
kings, 15, 20, 140, 145, 147, 150, 197
Knock, 304
knowledge, 8, 13, 18, 53, 99, 208

L

labor, 241
lack, 30, 125, 147, 247, 311
Lamb, 130
Law, 9

leadership, 14, 154
Leadership, 310, 314
legal arguments, 13
legal hearing, 13
lessons, 7
levels, 9, 141
liberty, 95, 96, 100
life-changing, 138, 283
light, 63, 75, 78, 124, 129, 138, 187, 198, 268, 273, 299, 311
lighting, 86
limitations, 1
listen, 3, 4, 8, 10, 11, 13, 15, 71, 93, 102, 125, 133, 138, 140, 141, 154, 160, 161, 166, 220, 249, 274, 292, 310, 312
listening, 1, 4, 10, 312
lonely, 175
Loose, 260, 267
Lord, 1, 2, 3, 4, 5, 6, 7, 8, 9, 10, 11, 12, 13, 14, 15, 17, 18, 19, 21, 22, 23, 24, 29, 30, 35, 36, 37, 38, 41, 42, 43, 44, 49, 50, 51, 55, 56, 57, 58, 59, 60, 61, 63, 64, 65, 70, 71, 72, 77, 78, 79, 81, 82, 85, 86, 92, 93, 95, 96, 98, 99, 100, 101, 102, 103,110, 111, 114, 116, 119, 120, 124, 125, 126, 131, 132, 133, 137, 138, 139, 140, 141, 144, 146, 147, 148, 153, 154, 157, 160, 161, 164, 166, 167, 171, 172, 173, 174, 175, 176, 181, 182, 186, 187, 188, 192, 193, 194, 198, 199, 200, 203, 204, 205, 208, 209, 214, 215, 219, 220, 221, 224, 225, 226, 227, 233, 237, 239, 240, 241, 242, 243, 244, 246, 247, 248, 249, 250, 255, 256, 260, 261, 262, 263, 267, 268, 269, 274, 275, 277, 278, 283, 284, 291, 292, 295, 298, 299, 300, 305, 306, 308, 310, 311, 312, 313, 314, 315
Lord of Lords, 139, 146, 181
loud, 1

love, 36, 37, 38, 43, 50, 59, 65, 107, 118, 125, 152, 166, 167, 169, 219, 220, 221, 223, 224, 226, 227, 244, 261, 283, 284, 299
Love, 165, 283
loving, 15, 37, 148, 178, 182, 227, 261, 288
low estate, 57
lust, 50, 51
lying, 37, 193

M

majesty, 9, 54
manifestation, 199
marriage, 30, 85
married couple, 29
marry, 29
mastered, 11
matchless, 277, 278
Matchless Savior, 275, 276
measure, 8, 20, 30, 119
mediator, 64
meditate, 12, 15, 54, 57, 138, 240, 275
mental images, 57
mercy, 5, 16, 256, 261, 263
message, 57, 63, 77, 79, 160, 262, 292
messenger, 78
Messiah the Prince, 242
mind, 5, 7, 78, 92, 93, 158, 160, 161, 173, 192, 198, 199, 211, 243, 298, 305, 315
minds, 120, 132, 141, 200, 208, 243, 284
minister, 100

ministers, 49
ministry, 14, 85, 101, 131, 220, 315
miracles, 92, 148, 206, 239, 315
miry clay, 36
misinterpret, 56
misunderstood, 1
morning, 16, 128, 220
Moses, 20, 21
mother's womb, 50, 110
motives, 176, 234
mountains, 305
mourns, 137
mouth, 1, 3, 17, 19, 20, 23, 100, 125, 138, 150, 199, 220, 243, 266, 299
murderous, 37
murky water, 23, 30, 44, 65, 284
music, 1, 2, 3, 4, 7, 24, 30, 44, 65, 71, 92, 140, 157, 214, 220, 243, 249, 269, 292, 299
mysteries, 8, 14, 137, 176, 233, 243

N

Name, 35, 42, 48, 63, 64, 103, 126, 130, 141, 180, 250, 292
nation, 60
nations, 19, 114, 116, 147, 197
naturally, 2, 8, 9, 36, 239
neck, 43, 65, 91, 226, 268
new season, 188
new streams, 15
noise, 11, 244, 291

notebooks, 239

O

obedience, 12, 98, 208
obey, 8, 9, 10, 138, 151, 152, 208, 240, 277
opinion, 208
opportunities, 220
opportunity, 85, 126, 131, 194
opposite, 226, 239
outcome, 278
overcome, 161, 187, 214, 310
overflow, 23, 30, 44, 65, 119
overwhelming, 102, 283

P

pain, 180, 181, 182, 227, 243, 262, 298
parables, 205
pastime, 166
pastors, 101
pastures, 4, 247
path, 5, 22, 34, 43, 70, 125, 269, 274, 275, 298
patient, 40, 56, 57, 135
Paul, 7, 131, 132
peace, 17, 18, 29, 62, 181, 208, 211, 212, 224, 243, 244, 298
perceive, 13, 18, 19, 55
perseverance, 136, 221
petition, 136, 261
Philistines, 9

Index

pictures, 57
plans, 4, 15, 86, 110, 246
pleasure, 7, 176, 234
pleasures, 22, 43, 70
plot, 306
poets, 43, 71
poor, 59, 95, 172, 193, 196, 283
position, 2, 9, 214, 269, 277, 311
possible, 2, 167, 215, 256
power, 3, 7, 9, 29, 37, 49, 65, 77, 81, 82, 86, 91, 99, 119, 132, 140, 180, 199, 204, 226, 243, 256, 299, 313, 314
powerful, 8, 202
practice, 4, 56
praise, 1, 3, 4, 10, 23, 30, 35, 42, 48, 51, 59, 71, 84, 96, 118, 119, 138, 139, 140, 174, 175, 199, 215, 237, 262, 269, 283, 288
pray, 14, 16, 61, 71, 106, 137, 141, 158, 161, 176, 182, 188, 194, 200, 209, 214, 221, 227, 234, 244, 256, 262, 269, 275, 278, 292, 300
Pray, 131, 136
prayed, 92, 175, 220, 265
prayer, 3, 4, 16, 17, 29, 40, 59, 78, 135, 136, 137, 138, 171, 187, 193, 199, 262
PRAYER, 23, 30, 37, 44, 50, 65, 72, 78, 86, 92, 102, 111, 119, 126, 132, 141, 148, 154, 161, 167, 176, 182, 187, 194, 200, 209, 215, 221, 227, 234, 244, 250, 256, 263, 269, 278, 284, 292, 299, 306
preach, 95, 96
preacher, 21
preaching, 138

presence, 2, 3, 5, 10, 22, 23, 24, 29, 30, 42, 43, 44, 46, 58, 64, 65, 70, 118, 119, 166, 171, 175, 243, 255, 256, 269, 314

prevail, 85

price, 182

pride, 50, 51

pride of life, 50, 51

Prince of Peace, 35, 36

principalities, 15

principality, 233

prison, 96

privilege, 14

problem, 56, 125, 138

proclaim, 3, 96, 119, 153, 161, 306

PROCLAMATIONS, 27, 34, 41, 47, 54, 69, 75, 82, 89, 96, 106, 116, 123, 129, 136, 145, 151, 158, 164, 170, 179, 185, 191, 197, 203, 212, 218, 224, 230, 237, 247, 253, 259, 266, 273, 281, 288, 296, 303, 309

profit, 62

promise, 120, 126, 260

promised, 3, 215, 262

promises, 29, 124, 260, 262, 315

promotion, 262

prophetic, 3, 7, 23, 30, 44, 65, 71, 78, 92, 132, 148, 153, 181, 193, 233, 277, 298, 315

prophets, 20, 101, 232

prosperity, 265

protected, 15

protection, 209, 298, 305

protector, 234, 248

Proverbs, 8, 145, 225, 226, 229, 246, 299

psalms, 153, 157
purification, 30, 44, 65
Purification, 28, 30
purify, 29
purpose, 33, 56, 57, 98, 102, 110, 111, 119, 161, 181, 311
pursue, 224, 313, 314
puzzle, 99

Q

quality, 198
queens, 15
questions, 86, 125, 205

R

radio, 220, 315
realms, 234
reasons, 14
rebellious, 19, 37
rebuke, 172
receivers, 57
redeemer, 269, 278
redemption, 174, 178, 220, 232
REFLECTION, 24, 31, 38, 44, 51, 66, 72, 79, 86, 93, 103, 111, 120, 126, 133, 141, 148, 155, 161, 167, 176, 182, 188, 194, 200, 209, 215, 221, 234, 244, 250, 256, 263, 278, 292, 300, 306
refuge, 249, 287, 288, 305
rejected, 288
rejection, 2, 37, 160, 161, 249

Rejoice Essential Magazine, 315
relationship, 8, 14, 71, 138, 181, 193, 263, 269, 311, 313
relationships, 1
Relax, 44
religious sector, 153
religious traditions, 137
remembrance, 60
renew, 14
repentance, 199
repented, 60
rescued, 276
rest, 28, 93, 132, 141, 180, 275, 281
revealing, 15, 103
revelation, 14, 71, 78, 99, 199
reverberates, 10
reverence, 29, 44, 65, 102, 122
reverences, 2
rich, 193, 226
Righteous, 63, 64
righteousness, 5, 16, 17, 77, 96, 102, 185, 224, 272, 298
rivers, 15, 193, 194
rod, 5
room, 22, 23, 28, 29, 44, 65, 71, 91, 187, 220, 226, 243, 249, 310
rooted, 13
rulers, 15, 151
rulers of darkness, 15
rushing, 191, 220, 291

S

sacrificing, 9
Safe Haven Women Outreach, 314
saints, 18, 101, 136, 151
salvation, 59, 176, 234, 242, 249, 255, 261, 280, 287, 298
Samuel, 9, 171, 172, 193, 240, 315
Savior Christ, 49
scorpions, 91
Scripture, 1, 3, 8, 15, 208, 233, 259
SCRIPTURE SUPPORT, 22, 28, 36, 42, 48, 64, 70, 76, 84, 90, 101, 110, 118, 124, 130, 139, 146, 152, 159, 165, 174, 180, 186, 192, 198, 207, 213, 219, 225, 232, 242, 248, 255, 260, 268, 277, 283, 291, 298, 304
secrets, 137
seed, 111
seeds, 4, 79
SELF-EVALUATION, 23, 30, 37, 44, 50, 65, 71, 78, 86, 92, 102, 111, 119, 125, 132, 141, 147, 154, 161, 167, 176, 181, 187, 194, 199, 209, 214, 220, 226, 233, 244, 250, 256, 262, 269, 278, 284, 292, 299, 306
selfishness, 14
serpents, 91
servant, 16, 23, 85, 96, 161, 172
serves, 23
shadows, 110, 248, 250
Shake, 267, 268, 269
shame, 2
shepherd, 4, 5, 247
shift, 15, 93, 132, 154, 214, 243, 244
shock, 147, 153, 277
shocker, 14

sight, 7, 10, 95, 166, 241
signs, 29, 92, 274
silence, 58
sin, 64, 81, 185
sing, 3, 5, 7, 44, 71, 132, 158, 288, 298, 305
singing, 3, 4, 5, 91, 92, 132, 153, 214, 233, 269, 278, 306
Sinners, 10
skills, 101
Soaring Wing Symposium, 208
sojourner, 17
song, 3, 4, 12, 23, 29, 30, 36, 37, 43, 44, 65, 71, 78, 85, 91, 92, 102, 110, 111, 119, 125, 126, 131, 132, 140, 148, 153, 160, 161, 167, 175, 181, 187, 188, 193, 194, 199, 200, 208, 209, 214, 215, 220, 221, 226, 227, 233, 243, 249, 250, 255, 256, 262, 269, 278, 283, 288, 292, 298, 299, 305, 306
soul, 4, 19, 35, 74, 91, 96, 111, 129, 159, 160, 176, 188, 192, 241, 244, 249, 263, 278, 283, 299, 306
sound, 2, 4, 13, 55, 57, 61, 63, 92, 98, 99, 138, 141, 204, 291, 292, 299, 310
sound of God, 4
sovereignty, 10, 151
speak, 3, 8, 9, 15, 18, 19, 21, 61, 72, 78, 148, 187, 188, 204, 205
speechless, 205
Spirit, 1, 11, 22, 24, 30, 44, 46, 65, 70, 86, 95, 96, 136, 137, 138, 148, 153, 160, 166, 173, 181, 187, 205, 206, 292, 310, 313, 315
spirit of heaviness, 96
Spirit of Power, 22
Spirit-filled, 1
spiritual plug, 15
spiritual songs, 153, 157

spiritually, 2, 9, 10
splendor, 1, 3, 54, 102
staff, 5
steadfast, 159, 211
steps, 5, 93, 133, 314
stomach, 175
stranger, 15, 17
stream, 193
strength, 59, 78, 79, 180, 181, 187, 188, 194, 283, 288, 298, 305
Strong's Concordance, 9
stronghold, 287, 298
struggle, 199, 233
studied, 56, 92, 111, 119, 132, 141, 148, 154, 161, 167, 175, 232
study, 7, 8, 14, 99
suffered, 37
suffering, 71, 85, 86, 147, 160, 181, 182
sufficient, 38, 85, 180, 184
sun, 272
supernaturally, 249
supplications, 16, 17, 59, 62
support, 44, 65
surrender, 14, 93, 132

T

table, 5
teachable, 154
teacher, 153, 315
teachers, 101

teaching, 14, 71, 72, 99, 102, 125, 132, 140, 153, 154, 166, 181, 199, 208, 256, 315

teachings, 312

tears, 17, 62, 131, 147, 226, 243

Tears, 91, 175

temple, 205

testimony, 13

thanks, 4, 6, 7, 118, 131, 150

Thanks, 130

thanksgiving, 288

thirst, 36, 173, 258

thoughts, 57, 244, 284

throne, 6, 7, 77, 85, 132, 274, 297

thunder, 8, 141, 291

time, 1, 2, 3, 4, 8, 12, 18, 33, 36, 37, 44, 50, 56, 62, 65, 78, 85, 86, 91, 92, 110, 137, 147, 160, 171, 175, 187, 204, 208, 239, 243, 249, 255, 256, 291, 292, 298, 312, 315

Timothy Ware Sr, 313

torment, 249

trace, 2

trained, 102, 239, 310, 311

transform, 9, 314

transforming, 3

transgression, 81

transmission, 72

trees, 10, 58, 96

tribulation, 40, 135

troubled, 84

troublesome, 242

trusted, 91, 175, 283

trusts, 211, 229
truth, 1, 2, 49, 69, 102, 103, 106, 110, 119, 140, 153, 173, 176, 263, 274, 312

U

unbelief, 37
undefeated, 86, 298
understand, 1, 8, 9, 11, 13, 18, 19, 50, 56, 57, 103, 110, 111, 205, 221, 226, 239, 242, 300
understanding, 2, 8, 99, 125, 176, 208, 215, 225, 233, 234, 284, 311, 315
unholy, 119
unknown, 141
unlovable, 227
usher, 3, 29, 119, 132, 311

V

vain repetitions, 61
valuable, 1, 166
variation, 71
vengeance, 96, 233
verify, 55
victories, 278
victorious, 277
victory, 77, 78, 79, 86, 120, 124, 214, 278, 292, 306
Victory, 76, 290, 291
vindicated, 147
vision, 8, 92, 131, 171, 233, 315

visitations, 78
vocation, 38
voice, 1, 5, 7, 8, 9, 10, 11, 14, 15, 16, 21, 58, 59, 60, 63, 78, 114, 171, 173, 187, 191, 193, 204, 205, 240, 243, 244, 269, 291, 295, 306, 310, 312

W

war, 84, 85, 306, 311
War, 83, 84, 86
warfare, 199, 239, 269
warring angel, 233
water, 5, 91, 92, 173, 190, 199, 202, 203, 255, 258, 259, 277, 284
waterfalls, 92
waters, 4, 8, 11, 91, 237, 247, 291, 295
weakness, 137, 180, 311
weapon, 23
weaponry, 299, 306
weapons, 86
Webster's Dictionary, 13
wickedness, 60, 298
wife, 10, 30, 58
willing vessel, 227
willingness, 138, 154, 256
Win, 76, 83, 84
winds, 43, 65, 109, 237, 249, 277
wisdom, 8, 59, 99, 153, 180, 215, 229, 234
wise, 18, 59, 226, 275
witness, 148, 173
witnesses, 20, 62, 85

wonder, 275, 276
Wonderful, 36, 297
wonders, 29, 92, 274
Word, 1, 2, 7, 8, 9, 10, 13, 30, 34, 49, 50, 55, 56, 63, 77, 83, 98, 99, 138, 175, 187, 232, 239, 256, 267, 306
Word of God, 10, 55, 77
world, 1, 2, 4, 9, 10, 19, 21, 49, 59, 61, 77, 86, 99, 102, 105, 106, 107, 111, 124, 137, 153, 155, 160, 161, 166, 173, 176, 187, 188, 204, 212, 213, 214, 226, 233, 234, 250, 255, 284, 299, 310, 312
worship, 3, 4, 8, 10, 23, 30, 37, 49, 50, 85, 92, 118, 119, 122, 138, 139, 171, 187, 192, 193, 215, 233, 243, 262, 269, 282, 305
Worship, 7, 118, 140, 192, 193, 267, 282
WORSHIP EXPRESSION, 23, 29, 36, 43, 49, 64, 71, 77, 85, 91, 101, 110, 119, 125, 131, 140, 147, 153, 160, 166, 175, 181, 187, 193, 199, 208, 214, 220, 226, 232, 243, 249, 255, 261, 268, 277, 283, 291, 298, 305
worshipper, 172
worshipping, 36, 92, 125, 175
worthy, 6, 7, 35, 37, 48, 51, 139, 199, 202, 215, 269
wrath, 21

Y

yoke, 60, 169

Z

zealous, 38
Zechariah, 77, 82, 268
Zolisha L Ware, 313, 316

Ears to Proclaim God's Splendor

www.ingramcontent.com/pod-product-compliance
Lightning Source LLC
Chambersburg PA
CBHW071954110526
44592CB00012B/1080